Small Feasts

Small Feasts

Soups, Salads & Sandwiches

Edited by Marilee Matteson

Clarkson N. Potter, Inc./Publishers NEW YORK

DISTRIBUTED BY CROWN PUBLISHERS, INC.

Clarkson N. Potter, Inc.
A division of Crown Publishers, Inc.
One Park Avenue
New York, New York 10016

Published simultaneously in Canada by
General Publishing Company Limited.
Printed in Japan by Toppan Printing Company

 created by Media Projects Incorporated
coordinating editor: Ellen Coffey
photography by Sally Andersen-Bruce
additional photographs by John Naso

Small Feasts.
  Includes index.
  1. Soups.   2. Salads.   3. Sandwiches.
I. Matteson, Marilee.
TX757.S55 1980   641.8   80-16347
ISBN 0-517-54052-5

Contents

Soups

ONE
Essentials & Extras

TWO
The Soups

Salads

ONE
Dressings & Green Salads

TWO
The Salads

Sandwiches
ONE
Essentials & Extras

TWO
The Sandwiches

Introduction

SMALL FEASTS was created with the help of culinary specialists Helen Barer, former editor of Time-Life Books' remarkable Foods of the World series; Pamela Geraldi Rabin, a respected food writer and radio commentator; Evie Righter, an associate editor at *Gourmet* magazine; and Elizabeth Esterling, founder of Paris Cooks school of gourmet cuisine in Washington, D.C.

SMALL FEASTS combines three separate cookbooks—Soups, Salads, and Sandwiches—in one volume. As you will see, the individual elements naturally fit with one another. However, each section stands completely on its own as an independent treatment of the subject at hand. Here are the ABC's of soups, salads, and sandwiches and then some: Each part has almost a hundred recipes; each is illustrated with photographs in full color; each contains recipes from celebrities and stars of the world of food. These include:`

Michael Batterberry, respected gourmet cook and connoisseur of wine, founder and editor-in-chief of *The International Review of Food & Wine*.

Milton Glaser, world-famous graphic designer and co-author of *The Underground Gourmet*, a guide to moderately-priced restaurants in New York City.

Michel Guérard, owner of the Michelin-starred Les Prés d'Eugénie restaurant in the South of France. A master of *cuisine minceur*, he has written several cookbooks, among them *Michel Guérard's Cuisine Minceur* and *Michel Guérard's Cuisine Gourmande*.

Joan Itoh, a weekly columnist for *The Japan Times*, and author of *Rice-Paddy Gourmet* and *Japanese Cooking Now*.

Mrs. Mary Janedis, whose authentic old-country recipe for traditional Greek lentil soup has been perfected over several generations.

Diana Kennedy, a highly respected authority on Mexican cooking and author of *The Cuisines of Mexico*, *The Tortilla Book*, and *Recipes from the Regional Cooks of Mexico*.

Old Denmark, a very fine Scandinavian restaurant and specialty food shop in New York City, famous for its open-face sandwiches.

Maurice Moore-Betty, author of several cookbooks, contributor to national food magazines, and teacher at the Moore-Betty School of Fine Cooking in New York City.

Guy Pascal, master *patissier* and owner of Manhattan's elegant French pastry shop, Délices la Côte Basque.

Jacques Pépin, former chef to General Charles de Gaulle and author of the acclaimed illustrated guides to cooking, *La Methode* and *La Technique*. Mr. Pepin was also associated with Time-Life's Foods of the World series.

W. Peter Prestcott, a well-known cook, caterer, and food stylist.

Richard Sax, chef, caterer, and food editor, and former overseer of the test kitchen at *The International Review of Food & Wine*.

Mimi Sheraton, renowned restaurant critic and food authority of *The New York Times* and author of several books, including *The German Cookbook* and *From My Mother's Kitchen*.

André Soltner, *chef-propriétaire* of the award-winning Lutèce restaurant in New York City.

Stella Standard, food writer, whose most recent books are *Our Daily Bread* and *The Stella Standard Soup Book*.

The Russian Tea Room, a famed gathering spot for authors, politicians, musicians, theater folk, and others of renown.

Miriam Ungerer, author of *Good Cheap Food*, and creator of many well-respected recipes.

Helen Witty, co-author with Elizabeth Schneider Colchie of *Better Than Store Bought* and frequent contributor to food magazines.

A feast means an array, a wealth of choice, a selection of special preparations. SMALL FEASTS is just such a collection, but it simplifies the often arduous task of creating a menu by gathering the recipes in one place. Discover, in the suggestions that follow, how a cup of soup, a salad, and a sandwich belong together, and serve quite splendidly as a complete meal—one that is tasty, satisfying, even sophisticated if the occasion requires, and not difficult to prepare. You can plan lunch, brunch, dinner, or supper. Be fancy. Be plain. Please children when you must, and delight guests when you wish.

If your whim is to evoke faraway places, do so. A menu of Cherry Soup, Potato Salad with Caraway Seed, and Old Denmark's Smoked Salmon Smørrebrød suggests a refreshing luncheon in Copenhagen's Tivoli Gardens. Fend off the miseries of a rainy day with a touch of France—Hot Potage Saint-Germain, Croque-Monsieur, and Beets in Mustard Dressing. Create your own fiesta with Gazpacho, Beef Tacos with Salsa Fria, Cherry Tomatoes with Avocado. And if deli food appeals, don't bother ordering out when you can make Matzoh Ball Soup, Coleslaw, Roast Beef on rye; some of the best of American fare.

SMALL FEASTS helps you to plan menus around seasons as well as countries. Think summer, for example, when you prepare Carrot Vichyssoise, Ratatouille Sandwiches, and Helen Witty's Remolded Broccoli Salad. Should it actually *be* summer, serve them in the backyard, or in the shade of a tall leafy elm. Announce spring when you pack your first picnic hamper of the season with elegant Cream of Asparagus Soup, Guy Pascal's Pâté Sandwiches, and Turkish Cucumber Salad. Watch the snow fall as you sit with friends around your kitchen table laid with Cheddar Cheese Soup, Hot Dogs with Baked Beans, and Green Salad with Mustard Yogurt Dressing. Celebrate the best of early fall with Mushroom Soup, the Classic Club Sandwich, and a Fresh Fruit Platter.

The culinary advice that states so emphatically hot soup must only be served with a hot meal and chilled soup only with a cold meal is outdated and will not be found in SMALL FEASTS. Times have changed. Your preferences and good sense should prevail. It goes without saying that on a hot summer afternoon you will hardly want to tend a steaming cauldron of vegetable soup. But the fresh taste of Gazpacho, for example, so right for summer, is just as enticing any time of the year.

The recipes in SMALL FEASTS, though diverse, have much in common. To begin with, they taste good, and most of them do not require extensive preparation. Then, too, each dish can stand on its own or be combined with others for a more substantial repast. You can fix these foods for yourself and enjoy them, or share them with a friend; prepare them for a large gathering, or compose your own all-celebrity menu in honor of your most cherished friends or relatives.

Today time is precious to most of us. We simply cannot devote hours to producing complicated and multi-course meals. But seldom have we recognized more clearly the importance of wholesome and healthy foods. It may be fashionable for us to eat less, but it is just as fashionable and intelligent to take what we eat seriously. For your own SMALL FEASTS you can bake your own breads, or create your own nutritious soups and salads. And once in a while, devote time to making such an extra-special dish as André Soltner's Seafood Ballottine Sandwiches. The result is your reward.

Most of all, have fun with SMALL FEASTS. Keep in mind that one definition of to feast is to delight in.

NOTE: A simple referral system cross-references recipes for use with one another. A recipe with capitals—for example, Smoked Salmon Butter—that appears in an introduction, ingredient list, note, or variation can be found in the index and easily located in the text.

Acknowledgments

The publishers acknowledge with gratitude the contribution of the following material that appears in this volume.

From *The International Review of Food & Wine:* Michael Batterberry's Fresh Tomato & Celery Salad, Sherried Orange Salad, Greek Salad Hero, Avocado-Shrimp Sandwiches, Artichoke Sandwiches; Milton Glaser's Chicken Salad Sandwiches; Maurice Moore-Betty's Curried Fish Pitas, Hot Vegetable Pitas; Old Denmark's Smoked Salmon Smørrebrød; Guy Pascal's Pâté Sandwiches; Jacques Pepin's Herbed Tomato Sandwiches; W. Peter Prestcott's Chlodnik, Simple Trimmed Vegetable Salad, Chicken Salad, Herring Sandwiches; Richard Sax's Hungarian Gulyas Soup, Cream of Cantaloupe Soup with Coconut & Ham, Warm Potato Salad with Scallions & Mustard, Rolled Ham Sandwiches, Ham & Cheese Sandwiches; Andre Soltner's Seafood Ballotine Sandwiches; Miriam Ungerer's "Poker Face from a Lady."

Through the courtesy of the following: Mrs. Mary Jandeis' Lentil Soup; Robert Quan's Winter Melon Soup; Pam Geraldi Rabin's Puree of Apple Soup; The Russian Tea Room's Hot Borscht; Stella Standard's Red Snapper Chowder and Stella Standard's Lamb Burgers.

The editorial and consulting services of the following individuals are acknowledged by the publishers and by the general editor of this volume: Helen Barer, Elizabeth Esterling, Pam Geraldi Rabin, and Evie Righter.

Menus

An Italian Sunday Night Supper
Stracciatella
Mozzarella in Carrozza
Onion & Tomato Salad

Hearty & Healthful from Greece
Avgolemono
Maurice Moore-Betty's Stuffed Pitas
Greek Salad

A Middle Eastern Refreshment
Middle Eastern Yogurt-Cucumber Soup
Felafel
Grape & Nut Salad

A Light French Luncheon
Jellied Madriléne
Brie & Vermouth Squares
Salade Niçoise

A Deli Lunch
Matzoh Ball Soup
Deli Numbers
Bread & Butter Pickles
Mimi Sheraton's Mother's Coleslaw

A Scandinavian Selection
Cherry Soup
Potato Salad with Caraway Seeds
Old Denmark's Smoked Salmon Smørrebrød

From Russia for Lunch
The Russian Tea Room's Hot Borscht
Sour Cream & Caviar Sandwiches
Succulent Cabbage Salad

With Spanish Overtones
Gazpacho
Cherry Tomatoes with Avocado
Beef Tacos with Salsa Fria

From the Shore
Moules Marinière
Salmon Mold
Watercress Tea Rolls

The Oriental Influence
Richard Quan's Winter Melon Soup
Michael Batterberry's Sherried Orange Salad
Mandarin Steak Sandwiches

An Italian Winter Luncheon
Minestrone
Basic Green Salad with Tarragon Vinaigrette
    Dressing
Garlicky Anchovy Toast

A French Autumn Luncheon
Hot Potage Saint-Germain
Croque-monsieur
Beets in Mustard Dressing

Simple & Sensational
Bouillabaise with Rouille
Basic Green Salad with Chive Vinaigrette
    Dressing
Fresh Herb Bread

Best of the Garden for Dinner
Carrot Vichysoisse
Helen Witty's Remolded Broccoli Salad
Ratatouille Sandwiches

A Hearty Lunch or Dinner
Black Bean Soup
Tiered Vegetable Salad
Basic Burgers

For the Kids
Tomato-Chive Soup
The Purist's Peanut Butter & Jelly Sandwich
Banana Split Salad

An Elegant Summer Luncheon
Cream of Sorrel Soup
Basic Shellfish Salad
Cucumber Rounds

For a Hot Summer Day
Minted Pea Soup
Curried Tuna in Melon Boats
Country Wheat Bread with Flavored Butters

A Stylish Picnic
Cream of Asparagus Soup
Turkish Cucumber Salad
Guy Pascal's Pâté Sandwiches

A La Nouvelle Cuisine
Consommé Brunoise
Duck & Orange Salad
Blue Cheese & Apple Slices

Sunday Brunch
Jellied Mushroom Soup
Eggs Benedict on English Muffins
Green Bean Salad

Fancy & Foolproof
Cream of Celery Soup
Chef's Salad with Russian or Green Goddess
    Dressing
Cuban White Bread with Flavored Butters

A Simple Inexpensive Picnic
Vichysoisse
Chilled Tomato-Orange Soup
Blueberry Soup
***
Cream Cheese & Olive Sandwiches
Meatloaf Sandwiches
Carrot & Apple Sandwiches
***
Potato Salad
Eggs Stuffed with Ham
Papayapple Salad

An After-the-Theater Supper
Chilled Purée de Cresson
Tartare Toasts
Wilted Lettuce Salad

Basic & Tasty
New England Clam Chowder
Tuna & Bean Salad
Apple Walnut Bread

For a Snowy Day
Cheddar Cheese Soup
Green Salad with Mustard Yogurt Dressing
Hot Dogs with Baked Beans

When It Blows
French Vegetable Soup
Grilled Cheddar & Tomato Sandwiches
Grilled Swiss & Zucchini Sandwiches
Whole Cranberry Salad

For All Seasons
Split Pea Soup
Homemade Country Pâté with Country Wheat
     Bread
Flavored Butters
Caesar Salad

It Comforts
French Mushroom Soup
The Classic Club
Fresh Fruit Platter

Simple & Good
Mrs. Janedis' Lentil Soup
Milton Glaser's Chicken Salad Sandwiches
24-Karat Salad

Soups

SMALL FEASTS *begins with Soups. A delicate broth or richly flavored cream soup is a good first course; and a hearty soup can be a meal in itself.*

The culinary arts have come a long way since cauldrons perched over open fires held simmering concoctions of meat, bones, wild greens and herbs. We now may use food processors and fine enamel and copper pots for soups made of vegetables, fish or shellfish, or even cheese or fruit, but the basic concept has remained the same.

Stock, or broth, is the essential ingredient for many hearty soups; you will find recipes here for stocks based on chicken, beef, vegetables, and fish. And it's only a step or two from stock to consommé or madrilene. Once you know the basics, you can make stock with cooking liquids you would not otherwise have used, such as the water in which vegetables have been cooked or seafood has been steamed.

You can easily learn the secrets of out-of-the-ordinary garnishes and accompaniments that lend so much to simple soups: Matzoh Balls or Dumplings to make a clear soup hearty; Crème Fraîche, Croutons, Pastry Puffs to make a simple soup elegant.

Soups from the Garden include some surprises—Cauliflower Soup, Cream of Carrot Soup, Peanut Soup—and sophisticated specialities, such as Tomato-Orange Soup, Cream of Sorrel or Cream of Parsley Soup, and Soupe au Pistou.

Soups from the Sea include such standards as New England Clam Chowder, Oyster Stew, and Lobster Bisque. Here also are such celebrated and elegant feasts as Bouillabaise and Moules Marinière. Some of these soups require a little extra time and effort, but you will agree they are worth it, when you consider that they are as elegant and delicious as any three-star gourmet meal.

Hearty Soups from all over the globe will keep you warm and content through the winter months. Richard Sax's Hungarian Gulyás Soup, Diana Kennedy's Gallina Pinta, The Russian Tea Room's Hot Borscht, and a luscious Cock-a-Leekie are perfect antidotes to cold, snowy days.

The joys of lighter, Summer Soups include Cream of Asparagus, Cucumber, Vichyssoise, Gazpacho, Swedish Fruit Soup. These summer soups can today be served year-round; the ingredients might be a little more expensive out of season, but these enjoyable soups themselves are always appropriate.

Soups are comforting, satisfying, refreshing. Among these are soups for every mood and occasion—for an elegant party or an intimate meal at home.

Black bean soup, tomato soup, minestrone, lentil soup

ONE
Essentials & Extras

The Stockpot

A fine soup stock is a foundation of good cooking the world over and can be created by even the most inexperienced of cooks. Further, rich homemade stock can be prepared and then left to simmer steadily on a back burner of the stove while the cook's attention is turned elsewhere.

Start with the best stockpot you can find. You'll need a covered, sturdy metal one large enough to hold soup bones, meat or poultry, vegetables, and from two to four quarts of water. Remember, you'll have to lift that brimming pot, so choose carefully for both weight and size.

Homemade stock is economical. Store the bones and trimmings from a roast or chicken in the freezer. Vegetable "scraps" from carrots, the tough ends of asparagus stalks, or zucchini trimmings are all good additions to the pot. So are celery tops, lettuce leaves, and the stem ends of parsley sprigs. Save the cooking liquid from fresh peas, summer squash, and any other delicately flavored vegetable: It can be substituted for water in many soup recipes.

Stocks and other soups routinely call for a bouquet garni. This little herb bouquet is made by tying together a bay leaf, fresh or dried thyme, and parsley sprigs. The quantities of herbs given in the following recipes are approximate and may be altered according to taste. Other ingredients that can be added to a bouquet garni include fennel, dried orange peel, and either fresh or dried herbs such as rosemary, tarragon and basil. If using dried thyme or other dried herbs, arrange them, the parsley, and bay leaf on a square of cheesecloth and tie the corners with kitchen string to create a small bag. If using fresh herbs in sprigs, simply tie them in a bunch. The bouquet garni is added to the pot with the first ingredients and will slowly release its flavor as the liquid simmers.

Canned chicken or beef broth can be substituted for homemade stock in most recipes. The taste will be different, for stock is flavored with vegetables and herbs while broth is simply the liquid from simmered meat or poultry. If you wish, you can turn a canned broth into a simple stock by simmering it for an hour with a few vegetables and a bouquet garni before straining it to use for soup.

Clarified stock to use as consommé or for transparent soups requires a minimum of time and effort to make but must be carefully handled. Start with a rich, homemade stock, either poultry or beef, and be sure that all the fat has been removed from the surface. Fat is easier to remove when the stock has been chilled to a gelatin-like consistency. Incidentally, all your equipment—saucepan, mixing bowl, whisk, spoon—must be thoroughly grease-free. Egg whites, absorbers of impurities, are part of the clarifying process and are added to the pot when the liquid is cold.

Chicken Stock

(2½-3 quarts)

- 3 pounds chicken parts, bones included, or 1 3-pound chicken
- 1½ pounds veal bones, cut into small pieces
- 2 carrots
- 2 medium onions, 1 studded with 3 cloves
- 1 stalk celery
- 6 peppercorns
- 1 teaspoon salt
- 16 cups cold water

Bouquet garni: 1 bay leaf, ½ teaspoon dried thyme, and 4 sprigs parsley

Put all the ingredients in a very large stockpot and bring the water slowly to a boil. Skim off the fat from the surface and simmer the mixture, partially covered, for 3 hours. (Stocks must be cooked slowly and never be allowed to boil or they will become cloudy.)

Remove the chicken and strain the stock through a fine sieve into a large bowl. Let the stock cool and skim off the fat again. Cover and refrigerate. Any remaining fat will solidify into a layer that can easily be removed when cold. Divide the stock among airtight containers and freeze it, or use it immediately.

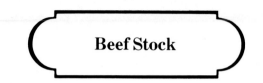

Beef Stock

(2 ½-3 quarts)

Follow the recipe for Chicken Stock, substituting 1½ pounds lean beef for the chicken parts and 1½ pounds beef bones, cut into small pieces, for the veal bones. Add 3 small white turnips and 3 leeks, cut into pieces.

Clarified Chicken or Beef Stock

(6-8 servings)

- 8 cups cold Chicken Stock or Beef Stock
- ¾ pound very lean chopped beef (optional)
- 2 egg whites
- 2 egg shells, wiped clean and crushed

Put the stock and the chopped beef, if desired, in a large stainless steel saucepan. In a small bowl beat the egg whites until frothy and add them to the stock. Add the egg shells. Place the pan over moderate heat and whisk constantly until the stock comes to a boil. When the egg whites have risen to the surface, remove the pan from the heat and let the mixture stand for 5 minutes. Return the pan to the heat, bring the liquid to a boil again, lower the heat, and simmer the mixture for 45 minutes. Be careful not to disturb the layer that forms on the stock; it will serve as a filter. Line a sieve with cheesecloth or a fine linen dish towel and gently pour the liquid through it into another pan. Hold back the filter layer in the stock until all the liquid has been strained and then let it slide into the sieve. Sieve the stock again through the filter layer and strainer. If the stock is not clear, repeat the procedure.

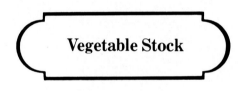

Vegetable Stock

(2 quarts)

1 tablespoon butter
1 pound onions, sliced
1 pound carrots, sliced
1 small white turnip, sliced
4 stalks celery with leaves, sliced
12 cups cold water
1 teaspoon salt
4 peppercorns
Bouquet garni: 1 bay leaf, ½ teaspoon dried thyme, and 5 sprigs parsley

Melt the butter in a very large stockpot over low heat. Add the vegetables and cook them until they are tender and brown. Add the water, salt, peppercorns, and bouquet garni and simmer the mixture, partially covered, for 1½ hours. Strain the stock through a fine sieve into a large bowl. Let the stock cool and skim off the fat from the surface. Cover and refrigerate. Divide the stock among airtight containers and freeze, or use immediately.

White Fish Stock

(4 quarts)

3 medium onions, thinly sliced
8 sprigs parsley
1 bay leaf
Juice of 1 lemon
4 pounds lean white fish trimmings, bones and heads included, but not gills
2 cups dry white wine
16 cups cold water
Salt

Put the onions, parsley, bay leaf, lemon juice, fish trimmings, and wine in a very large enamel or stainless steel stockpot and bring the liquid to a boil. Simmer the mixture, covered, for 10 minutes, add the water, and bring the mixture to a simmer. Skim off the froth from the surface and simmer the stock for 30 minutes. Strain the stock through a fine sieve and season to taste with the salt. Divide the stock among airtight containers and freeze it, or use it immediately.

Garnishes & Accompaniments

A variety of attractive garnishes are suggested to enhance and complement the flavors of the soups in this section. A sprinkling of minced parsley, bits of chopped scallion and chives, a scattering of buttery, toasted almonds, dabs of whipped cream and sour cream, and swirls of heavy cream appeal not only to the palate but also to the eye.

One of the richest and most delicious garnishes is *Créme Fraîche*, a secret from the kitchens of French chefs. You can find this luscious topping on strawberries, raspberries, and pastries, as well as dolloped on full-bodied vegetable and meat soups. The version here, a combination of sweet and sour cream, is easy to make, but must be allowed to rest several days to develop its distinctive nutty flavor.

Light-as-air dumplings afloat in a bowl of broth or clear chicken soup are the stuff of culinary fantasies but are not always simple to make. Here are a couple of hints for making this garnish:

Heat the soup in which the dumplings are to be cooked in a pot wide enough to accommodate all of them without crowding. When all the balls have been added, reduce the heat and simmer the soup, tightly covered.

Dumplings toughen when exposed to air, so resist the temptation to lift the lid and peek into the pot until the entire cooking period is completed. If your curiosity is absolutely unrestrainable, you might try using a glass pot cover.

Homemade croutons are another appealing garnish that will add flavor and texture to almost any kind of soup and can be seasoned with a variety of combinations. For a basic herb-garlic blend, brown the cubes in a good, fruity olive oil with garlic, then add pinches of basil and oregano. Float the croutons on a plateful of rich, Italian-style beef broth made with tomatoes. Instead of butter or oil, you can brown the croutons in drippings from meat or poultry. Bacon drippings, for instance, add a distinctive flavor to croutons served with a pea soup that is also sprinkled with sliced frankfurters.

Savory little pastry puffs, another creative idea from France, make elegant garnishes for special dinners. For a festive accompaniment to a clear soup, split the cooled pastry puffs and fill them with a dollop of shrimp paste or chicken liver pâté or a frothy blend of sour cream, blue cheese, and cream cheese.

Crème Fraîche

(2 cups)

1 cup heavy cream
1 cup sour cream

In a bowl mix the heavy cream with the sour cream until well blended. Cover and let stand at room temperature overnight. Stir and refrigerate for 8 hours before using.
Crème fraîche keeps covered in the refrigerator for at least a week. Use as a garnish on soups as well as on stews and on fresh fruit.

NOTE: Soup to which Crème Fraîche has been added can be brought to a boil without danger of curdling.

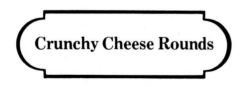

Crunchy Cheese Rounds

(Approximately 50)

½ pound butter or margarine, softened
2 cups grated sharp Cheddar cheese
2 cups sifted all-purpose flour
2 cups Rice Krispies
½ teaspoon salt
Pinch cayenne

Preheat the oven to 375°.
In a large bowl combine all the ingredients and blend them well. Form the mixture into small balls with a teaspoon, place them on ungreased cookie sheets, and press the top of each with a fork. Bake the rounds for 15 minutes and serve them hot. (These can be frozen in airtight containers and reheated.)

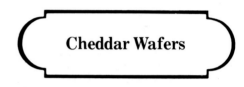

Cheddar Wafers

(Approximately 3 dozen)

¼ pound butter, softened
⅔ cup sifted all-purpose flour
½ pound extra sharp Cheddar cheese, grated
Worcestershire sauce
Hot pepper sauce

In a bowl blend the butter, flour, and cheese and add a few drops Worchestershire sauce and a drop of hot pepper sauce, or to taste. Shape the dough into a ball and turn it out onto a lightly floured surface. Form the dough into long logs about 1 inch thick, wrap them in waxed paper or foil, and chill them until firm. (The logs may be frozen at this point for later use.)
Preheat the oven to 450°.
Cut the chilled dough into ¼-inch slices, place them on ungreased cookie sheets, and bake them for 10 minutes. Let the wafers cool before serving.

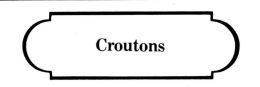

Croutons

(Approximately 1 cup)

- 3 thick slices firm white bread, with crusts removed
- 3 tablespoons vegetable oil
- 3 tablespoons butter
- Salt

Cut the bread into ½-inch squares. Heat butter and oil in a skillet and brown the cubes on all sides over moderate heat. Remove the croutons with a slotted spoon to drain on paper towels. Sprinkle with salt to taste.

HERB CROUTONS: Sprinkle a teaspoon of freshly chopped herbs such as parsley, tarragon, basil, oregano, or dill or a combination of same on the bread cubes in the skillet at the end of the cooking time.

GARLIC CROUTONS: Chop 1 clove garlic very fine and add it to the butter and oil in the skillet before adding the bread cubes.

CHEESE CROUTONS: Sprinkle hot croutons with freshly grated Gruyère, Cheddar, or fresh Parmesan cheese.

Pastry Puffs

(Approximately 3 dozen)

- 4 tablespoons butter
- ½ cup water
- ½ cup sifted all-purpose flour
- Pinch salt
- 2 eggs

Preheat the oven to 375°.

In a small saucepan melt the butter in the water and bring the liquid to a boil. Remove the pan from the heat and add the flour and salt all at once. Stir vigorously until the dough is smooth and pulls away from the sides of the pan. Cool the dough for 5 minutes and mix in the eggs, 1 at a time. Beat until the dough is smooth and shiny.

Form mounds of dough, ½ teaspoon at a time, or use a pastry bag fitted with a ¼-inch plain tube on a moistened cookie sheet. Bake the puffs for 20 minutes. Let the puffs cool before serving. (They freeze well in an airtight container.)

CHEESE PUFFS: After mixing in the eggs, add 3 tablespoons freshly grated Parmesan or Gruyère cheese and beat the mixture until dough is smooth and shiny. Proceed as in the master recipe.

Melba Toast

(8 pieces)

    4 very thin slices homemade-style white bread, with crusts removed

Preheat the oven to 350°.

    Cut each slice of bread in half and place the halves on an ungreased cookie sheet. Bake for 30 minutes, or until golden. To keep fresh and crisp, store the toast in an airtight container.

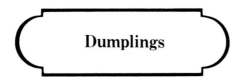

Dumplings

(Approximately 1 dozen)

    4 tablespoons butter, softened
    1 egg
    1 cup sifted all-purpose flour
  ⅛ teaspoon salt
    6 tablespoons milk
    4 cups Chicken Stock, Beef Stock, or canned chicken or beef broth

In a bowl beat together the butter and egg until smooth and blend in the flour and salt. Stir in the milk, a little at a time, and continue stirring until the dough is smooth.

Form the dough into small balls with a teaspoon and keep the balls covered with a damp towel.

    In a saucepan bring the stock or broth to a boil and while it is boiling, drop in the dumplings. (Dumplings expand during cooking, so don't crowd them.) Simmer the mixture, covered, for 10 minutes. Test the dumplings for doneness by inserting a toothpick in the middle of one. The pick will come out clean if the dumpling is done.

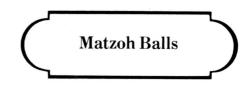

Matzoh Balls

(About 1 dozen)

    4 large eggs
  ½ teaspoon salt
Freshly ground white pepper
  ⅓ cup vegetable oil
  ½ cup water
 1¼ cups matzoh meal or finely crumbled matzoh crackers

In a bowl combine the eggs, salt, and pepper and beat to blend the ingredients. Beat in the oil, water, and matzoh meal. Chill the mixture, covered, 1 hour or overnight. Shape the chilled mixture into 1-inch balls and drop into boiling soup. Reduce the heat and simmer the matzoh balls for 30 minutes. Serve 1 or more matzoh balls in each bowl of soup.

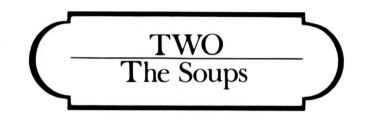

TWO
The Soups

Clear Soups

The shimmering purity of a consommé is a dramatic beginning for a sophisticated meal. Made by clarifying particularly rich Beef or Chicken Stock, such crystal clear soups should—according to purists—be served unadorned. Some very good cooks, however, use garnishes—rice, interestingly-shaped pastas, or, as in Consommé Brunoise, finely diced vegetables that are always cooked separately. And some cooks find nothing sacrilegious at all in passing a bowl of croutons with the consommé.

The Japanese are masters of the transparently clear soup. The rich flavor of dashi, the classic and superbly uncomplicated soup stock of Japan, contributes a distinctive taste to many of their traditional meals. Try recreating the gustatory as well as esthetic experience of dining in Japan where the appearance of food and the ceremony surrounding its presentation are as beautiful as a work of art. Serve the Japanese soups in this chapter in individual lacquer or porcelain bowls. No soup spoons are necessary— the Japanese drink soup from the bowl and eat the delicately shaped bits of vegetables, bean curd, meat, or fish that accompany it with chopsticks. The only difficulty you may encounter in preparing such soups is in finding the katsuobushi (dried bonito fillet) and dashi-kombu (seaweed). For those who do not have access to a market that stocks oriental foodstuffs, two mail-order suppliers are listed below:

Katagiri and Co.
224 East 59th St.
New York, N.Y.
10022

Japan Food Corp.
900 Marin Street
San Francisco, CA
94124

Clarified stock is used only when the cook wishes the final result to be crystal clear. Many other clear soups, equally light but less transparent, can be made with plain stock or broth. For the soup in this chapter called Stracciatella (ragged one), Italian cooks start with a chicken stock then add a frothy mixture of eggs, mellow Parmesan cheese, and fresh basil and parsley, all of which forms shreds. An unconventional but pleasing addition would be a garnish of toasted, buttered bread crumbs. And pass the Parmesan, please.

Joan Itoh's Shrimp & Daikon Soup

(4 servings)

    ¾ cup finely chopped cooked shrimp
    ½ teaspoon sugar
    Salt
    1 egg, beaten
    1 cup very finely cubed *daikon*
       (Oriental white radish)
    2 tablespoons *sake* (rice wine)
    8 mushrooms (*shiitake*)
    ¼ cup spinach leaves
    4 cups Basic Dashi
    Shoyu (Japanese soy sauce)

In a small bowl combine the shrimp, sugar, a pinch of salt, and the egg and mix thoroughly. Sprinkle the *daikon* with *sake* and salt and add to the shrimp mixture.

In a saucepan cook the mushrooms and spinach in a small amount of *dashi* and reserve, covered. In another saucepan bring the remaining *dashi* to a boil and season with *shoyu* to taste. Put a portion of the shrimp mixture, 2 mushrooms, and a spoonful of spinach in each soup bowl. Pour the boiling stock over the mixture and cover each bowl with a lid. The shrimp mixture will poach quickly in the hot liquid. Serve with the bowls still covered.

NOTE: This recipe is designed for soup bowls with lids. If you do not have this kind of bowl, poach the shrimp mixture separately for 1 minute in *dashi* to cover, and reserve until you are ready to assemble the soup in bowls.

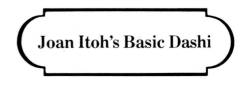

Joan Itoh's Basic Dashi

(4-6 servings)

    1 piece *dashi-kombu* (seaweed), about 4
       inches long
    1 ounce (approximately) *katsuobushi*
       (dried bonito fillet) shavings
    5 cups water

Wipe the *kombu* with a damp cloth and cut several slits in it with scissors. (The flavor will steep out of the slits into the soup.) In a saucepan place the *kombu* in the water and just before the water boils, take the *kombu* out and throw it away. Add a little cold water to keep the broth from boiling and add the *katsuobushi*. When the broth comes just to the boil, turn off the heat. Do not let the broth boil. After the shavings sink to the bottom, spoon the broth off and strain it carefully.

Grandmother's Chicken Soup

(6 to 8 servings)

6-8 whole chicken breasts with ribs, rinsed
10 cups water
1 teaspoon salt
2 medium carrots, grated fine
1 medium parsnip, grated fine
1 medium onion, finely minced
1 stalk celery, with leaves
Bouquet garni: 1 bay leaf, 1 peeled garlic clove, 10 black peppercorns, ⅛ teaspoon dried thyme, 2 cloves, 1 teaspoon dried parsley, 2 teaspoons grated parsnip
3-4 sprigs parsley
Matzoh Balls or cooked noodles

Put the chicken breasts (including the skin and fat) in a soup pot and add the water and salt. Add the carrots, parsnip, minced onion, celery stalk, and the bouquet garni, bring the water to a boil, and slowly simmer the mixture, partially covered, for 1 hour. Continue simmering for another 30 to 45 minutes uncovered.

Remove the chicken breasts and reserve them for another use. Remove and discard the celery and the bouquet garni. Allow the soup to cool. Pour into jars and let stand to cool further, then cap them and refrigerate the soup for a few hours, preferably overnight.

Skim from the soup almost all the fat that has risen to the top and hardened. Strain the soup into a soup pot, snip the leaves of the parsley sprigs into it, and reheat it. It should be steaming hot. Serve over matzoh balls or noodles.

NOTE: This soup is ideal for traditional Jewish holiday meals. You can bake the chicken breasts for a short time with a fruited glaze, as this Grandmother did, for an appealing and festive second entrée at a family gathering.

Stracciatella (Italian Chicken Soup)

(4-6 servings)

5 cups Chicken Stock or canned chicken broth
2 eggs
1 teaspoon chopped fresh basil
1 teaspoon chopped parsley
¼ cup freshly grated Parmesan cheese
Salt

In a large saucepan bring the stock or broth to a boil. In a small bowl whisk together the eggs, basil, parsley, and cheese, add salt to taste, and whisk the mixture into the stock. Continue stirring for 2 minutes. Serve the soup immediately in warmed bowls.

Jellied Mushroom Soup

(4 servings)

4 cups Clarified Chicken Stock
1 pound mushrooms, chopped
1 tablespoon unflavored gelatin
½ cup cold water
1 tablespoon dry sherry
½ teaspoon salt
Freshly ground black pepper
Sour cream
Chopped parsley

In a large saucepan bring the chicken stock to a simmer and add the mushrooms. Simmer the mixture for 30 minutes. Sprinkle the gelatin onto ½ cup cold water to soften. Strain the soup into another pan and stir in the softened gelatin, stirring until it is dissolved. Add the sherry and salt and season with pepper to taste. Chill for at least 8 hours. Garnish with dollops of sour cream, sprinkle with parsley, and serve.

Consommé Brunoise

(4 servings)

1 tablespoon butter
1 tablespoon diced carrot
1 tablespoon diced celery
1 tablespoon diced white turnip
1 tablespoon diced string beans
4 cups Clarified Chicken Stock or Beef Stock
Croutons

In a skillet melt the butter and cook the vegetables over low heat until they are tender but not brown. In a large saucepan add them to the stock, heat the mixture through, and serve it immediately. Garnish with croutons.

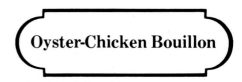

Oyster-Chicken Bouillon

(16 servings)

1 pint shucked oysters, minced
4 cups milk
16 cups Chicken Stock or canned chicken broth
2 tablespoons butter
Salt and freshly ground white pepper

In a very large soup pot combine the milk, stock or broth, and butter and heat the mixture through. Add the oysters and cook the soup over low heat for 10 minutes until the oysters are just firm. Season with salt and pepper to taste and serve the bouillon with oyster crackers.

Old-fashioned Jellied Madrilène

(4-6 servings)

1 28-ounce can tomatoes
6 cups Clarified Chicken Stock
1 medium onion, sliced
1 stalk celery with leaves, chopped
4 sprigs parsley
1 bay leaf
1 sprig fresh thyme or ½ teaspoon dried
5 fresh basil leaves or ½ teaspoon dried
Freshly ground black pepper
½ lemon
2 tablespoons unflavored gelatin
Salt
Chopped parsley
Lemon wedges

Put the tomatoes, stock, onion, celery, parsley, and herbs in an enamel or stainless steel soup pot and season the mixture with pepper to taste. Squeeze the lemon, add the juice and the lemon to the pot, and simmer the soup for 45 minutes. Sprinkle the gelatin onto ½ cup cold water to soften. Strain the soup into another pot and stir in the softened gelatin, stirring until it is dissolved. Add salt to taste. Chill the jellied madrilène for at least 8 hours. Serve in chilled bowls, sprinkle with parsley, and garnish with lemon wedges.

NOTE: To serve this soup hot, omit the gelatin from the preparation.

Soups from the Garden

Your table can bloom with all the colors of a country garden, from the subtle tints of cream-colored cauliflower and leaf-green romaine to carrot-orange and shades of tomato red. Use contrast—Crème Fraîche sprinkled with brown nutmeg atop jade green spinach soup. Invoke autumn with heavy sweet cream swirled into russet-colored pumpkin soup. Melt a pat of golden butter in the center of the swirl.

As the colors of these soups range from muted to vivid, so do their flavors. Cream of Lettuce Soup has such a subtle taste that your family and guests may not be able to identify the main ingredient. Soupe au Pistou, a bouquet of flavors from Provence, is redolent with garlic and basil. Pistou, a sauce made separately from the soup, is first cousin to the pesto sauce from Italy's Ligurian coast. That uncooked green sauce is ladled lavishly over bowls of pasta or spooned, rather more discreetly, into vegetable soups.

Many of the green soups you'll encounter in this chapter are of European ancestry— Potage Saint-Germain, the lettuce, spinach, parsley, and sorrel soups. In France, sorrel doubles as a salad green and potherb. Look for bunches of this pungent, arrow-shaped green in the spring and summer at ethnic markets and specialty shops. The leaves should be crisp and bright green. Use the smallest and tenderest sprigs in salads and the larger, tougher leaves in soups.

Peanuts, pumpkins, and little white turnips are all-American ingredients but the soups based on these vegetables can be a real surprise for the American table.

The recipes for these and other smooth soups almost always call for puréeing ingredients in a food mill, blender, or food processor. A food mill is preferable because it not only strains the soup as it purées but achieves a coarser texture than either a blender or processor.

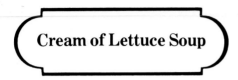

Cream of Lettuce Soup

(4 servings)

2   pounds romaine lettuce
½   cup green peas, fresh or frozen
6   tablespoons butter
½   cup minced scallions
Salt and freshly ground black pepper
4   tablespoons all-purpose flour
4   cups Chicken Stock or canned chicken
    broth (*see* Note), heated
Fresh chervil
1   cup heavy cream
Salted whipped cream

Coarsely chop and blanch the lettuce in a large quantity of boiling salted water for about 10 minutes, or until it is wilted. Toward the end of the cooking time, add the peas and cook them until tender. Drain the mixture. In a large saucepan melt the butter and cook the scallions until they are soft, add the lettuce, peas, and salt and pepper to taste, and cook, stirring for 2 to 3 minutes. Stir in the flour and cook, stirring, for 1 to 2 minutes. Stir in the stock or broth and adjust the seasonings. Purée the mixture in a food mill, blender, or food processor, 2 to 2½ cups at a time, until it is smooth. Add a generous pinch of chervil. Return the soup to the pan and blend in the cream. Reheat it if serving hot (or chill it if serving cold) and garnish each bowl with dollops of whipped cream.

NOTE: If using canned chicken broth, simmer first for 20 minutes with ½ cup each thinly sliced carrots and onions, 4 sprigs parsley, a big pinch of dried thyme, and ¼ cup dry white wine. Strain and proceed as above.

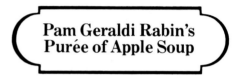

Pam Geraldi Rabin's Purée of Apple Soup

(4-6 servings)

3   tablespoons butter
1   small onion, finely chopped
5   apples, unpeeled, cored, and sliced
Salt and freshly ground white pepper
3   cups beef broth
3   tablespoons dry sherry
1   teaspoon arrowroot, mixed with 1
    tablespoon water
¼   cup blanched, sliced almonds, sautéed
    in 1½ teaspoons butter

In a large saucepan melt the butter and cook the onion until it is golden. Add the apple slices and salt and pepper to taste and cook the mixture until the apples are tender. Add the broth and sherry, bring to a boil, and simmer for 15 minutes. Stir in the arrowroot mixture and heat the soup, stirring, until it is thickened. Adjust the seasonings. Strain the soup through a fine sieve into another pan and reheat it. Serve the soup in warmed bowls and sprinkle with the almonds.

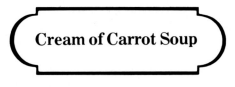

Cream of Carrot Soup

(4-6 servings)

      2   tablespoons butter
      ½   cup finely chopped onions
      4   cups Chicken Stock or canned chicken
           broth
      8   medium carrots, finely chopped
           (approximately 3 cups)
      2   tablespoons uncooked rice
      1   tablespoon tomato paste
      ½   cup heavy cream
Salt and freshly ground black pepper
Chopped parsley

In a large saucepan melt the butter and cook the onion until it is tender but not brown. Add the stock or broth, carrots, rice, and tomato paste and simmer the mixture, uncovered, for 30 minutes, or until the vegetables are tender. Purée the mixture in a food mill, blender, or food processor. Rinse the pan, return the soup to it, and add the cream and salt and pepper to taste. Reheat the soup and serve it in warmed bowls. Sprinkle with parsley.

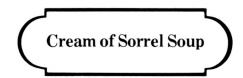

Cream of Sorrel Soup

(4-5 servings)

      2   teaspoons butter
      1   medium onion, finely chopped
      1   cup firmly packed shredded,
           deribbed sorrel
     2½   cups Chicken Stock or canned
           chicken broth
      3   egg yolks
      1   cup heavy cream
Salt and freshly ground black pepper

In a large saucepan melt the butter and cook the onion until it is tender but not brown. Add the sorrel and the stock or broth, bring the liquid to a boil, and simmer it, covered, for 5 minutes. Just before serving, stir in egg yolks that have been lightly beaten with the cream. Season the soup with salt and pepper to taste, reheat it, but do not let it boil.

Onion Soup

(4-6 servings)

- 2 tablespoons butter
- 4 medium onions, thinly sliced
- 1 teaspoon all-purpose flour
- 6 cups Beef Stock or beef bouillon made from 4 cubes with 6 cups water, heated
- ½ cup dry red or dry white wine (optional)

Salt and freshly ground black pepper
- 6 slices French bread, lightly toasted
- 3 tablespoons grated Gruyère cheese

In a large saucepan melt the butter and cook the onions until they are golden. Stir in the flour and cook, stirring, for 5 minutes. Stir in the stock or bouillon, add wine, if desired, and season with salt and pepper to taste. Simmer, partially covered, for 30 minutes. Adjust the seasoning as desired. Place the bread slices in the bottom of a casserole or in individual ovenproof bowls and pour in the soup. Sprinkle grated cheese over the bread and put the casserole or bowls in a hot oven or under the broiler until the cheese is melted. Or put a slice of bread in each bowl, sprinkle it with grated cheese, and pour the hot soup over it. The bread will rise to the surface.

Potage Parmentier
(Potato & Onion Soup)

(10-12 servings)

- 4 cups chopped onions
- 4 cups chopped potatoes
- 5 sprigs parsley
- 10 cups Chicken Stock, canned chicken broth, or chicken bouillon made from 10 cubes with 10 cups hot water
- 1½ cups milk

Salt and freshly ground white pepper
- ½ cup heavy cream (optional)

Chopped parsley or fresh chives

In a soup pot simmer the onions, potatoes, and parsley in the stock, broth, or bouillon, until the vegetables are tender. Purée the mixture in a food mill, blender, or food processor. Rinse the pan, return the soup to it, and add the milk. Season with salt and pepper to taste. Just before serving, add the cream if desired. Sprinkle each serving with parsley or chives.

Potage Saint-Germain (Cream of Pea Soup)

(6 servings)

    4   tablespoons butter
    1   teaspoon chopped onion
    4   tablespoons all-purpose flour
    2   cups milk
    2   cups Chicken Stock or canned chicken
        broth
    1   sprig fresh thyme or ¼ teaspoon
        dried
    4   sprigs parsley
    ¼   teaspoon grated nutmeg
Freshly ground black pepper
    4   cups peas, fresh or frozen
Salt
    ½   cup light cream

In a large saucepan melt the butter and cook the onion until it is tender but not brown. Stir in the flour and cook, stirring, for 1 minute. Stir in the milk, stir until thickened, and add the stock or broth, thyme, parsley, nutmeg, and pepper to taste. Cook the soup for 5 minutes, add the peas, and cook for 5 minutes more, or until they are tender. Purée the mixture in a food mill, blender, or food processor. Rinse the pan and return the soup to it. Before serving, season the soup with salt to taste, add the cream, and heat the soup through but do not let it boil.

Cream of Parsley Soup

(8 servings)

    3   tablespoons butter
    ⅓   cup minced shallots
    3   medium potatoes, sliced
    4   cups Chicken Stock or canned
         chicken broth
    1¼   cups firmly packed chopped celery
    1   or more cups light cream
Salt and freshly ground white pepper
    2½   tablespoons sour cream
Chopped fresh chives or parsley

In a large saucepan melt the butter and cook the shallots until they are tender. Add the potatoes and stock or broth. Bring the liquid to a boil and simmer it, covered, until the potatoes are tender. Let cool slightly and add the parsley. Purée the mixture in a food mill, blender, or food processor. Rinse the pan and return the soup to it. Stir in the cream, adding more if soup is too thick, and season with salt and pepper to taste. Serve the soup hot or cold. Garnish with sour cream and sprinkle it with chives or parsley.

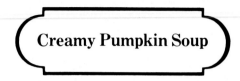

Creamy Pumpkin Soup

(6 servings)

2 tablespoons butter
1 medium onion, finely chopped
4 cups peeled, chopped pumpkin meat
   or canned pumpkin (unsweetened)
1 large potato, diced
2 medium tomatoes, peeled, seeded, and
   chopped
4 cups Chicken Stock, canned chicken
   broth, *or* water
Salt
Freshly ground black pepper
Hot pepper sauce
Chopped celery leaves
Chopped parsley
2 tablespoons butter
Light cream
Croutons

In a soup pot melt the butter and cook the onion until it is tender but not brown. Add the vegetables and the stock or broth.. Season with salt, pepper, hot pepper sauce, celery leaves, and fresh parsley to taste. Cook the vegetables until they are tender. Purée the mixture in a food mill, blender, or food processor. Rinse the pot and return the soup to it. Add the butter and cream, as desired,

and heat through. Serve the soup with croutons.

NOTE: For a festive presentation, serve this soup in a hollowed-out pumpkin.

Potage Freneuse (Turnip Soup)

(6 servings)

1 pound small white turnips, quartered
1 medium onion, quartered
Salt
3 tablespoons butter
2 tablespoons all-purpose flour
5 cups Chicken Stock, canned chicken
   broth, or chicken bouillon made from
   5 cubes with 5 cups water
2 egg yolks
2 tablespoons heavy cream, *or* Crème
   Fraîche
Freshly ground black pepper
Chopped chives

In a large saucepan melt the butter, stir in the flour, and cook, stirring, over low heat for 5 minutes. Stir in the stock, broth, or bouillon and bring the mixture to a boil, stirring until it is thickened. Add the turnips and onions and cook for 30 to 40 minutes until they are tender. Purée the mixture in a food mill, blender, or food processor. Rinse the pan and return the soup to it. Reheat the soup.

In a small bowl beat together the egg yolks and cream and slowly stir them into the warm soup. Whisk constantly until the soup thickens slightly. Do not let the soup boil or the eggs will scramble. Sprinkle with chives and serve.

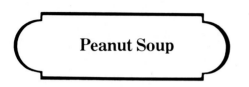

Peanut Soup

(6 servings)

2 stalks celery, finely chopped
1 small onion, finely chopped
4 tablespoons butter
2 tablespoons all-purpose flour
2 cups Chicken Stock or canned chicken broth
1 cup milk
1 cup light cream
1 cup smooth peanut butter
Salt and freshly ground black pepper
Paprika

In a large saucepan melt the butter and cook the celery and onion until lightly brown. Stir in the flour and cook, stirring, for 1 minute. Stir in the stock or broth and stir until soup boils and thickens. Add the milk and cream, return the soup to a boil, and simmer it for 5 minutes. Strain the soup and return it to the pan. Stir in the peanut butter, bring to a boil, and simmer for 5 minutes. Add salt and pepper to taste. Sprinkle with paprika and serve.

Spinach Soup

(6 servings)

2 pounds spinach or 2 packages thawed frozen spinach, finely chopped
3 tablespoons butter
Grated nutmeg
3 tablespoons all-purpose flour
6 cups Chicken Stock or canned chicken broth
Salt and freshly ground black pepper
Fresh lemon juice
Crème Fraîche

In a large saucepan melt the butter and cook the spinach with a pinch of nutmeg until it wilts. Sprinkle the mixture with the flour and cook for 1 minute. Stir in the stock or broth and stir until it is thickened. Purée the mixture in a food mill, blender, or food processor. Rinse the pan and return the soup to it. Add salt, pepper, and lemon juice to taste. Serve the soup hot or cold, sprinkle with nutmeg, and garnish with dollops of crème fraîche.

Tomato-Orange Soup

(6-8 servings)

2 pounds tomatoes, quartered, or
  1 28-ounce can drained
1 medium carrot, thinly sliced
1 medium onion, thinly sliced
1 bay leaf
1 lemon, thinly sliced
1 orange, thinly sliced
5 peppercorns
1 cup fresh orange juice
4 cups Chicken Stock or canned chicken
  broth
Salt
3 tablespoons butter
3 tablespoons all-purpose flour
Sugar
¾ cup heavy cream, whipped, *or* Crème
  Fraîche
Thin orange slices

Put the tomatoes in a large enamel or stainless steel saucepan and add the carrot, onion, bay leaf, lemon slices, orange slices, peppercorns, orange juice, stock or broth, and salt to taste. Bring the mixture to a boil and simmer it, uncovered, for 1 hour. Strain the soup through a fine sieve. Rinse the pan and over low heat melt the butter. Stir in the flour and cook, stirring, for 1 minute. Return the soup to the pan, bring it to a boil, and simmer for 5 minutes, or until it is thickened.

Add a little sugar to taste. Serve the soup hot or cold and garnish with whipped cream or Crème Fraîche and orange slices.

Soupe au Pistou (Provençal Vegetable Soup with Garlic)

(8-10 servings)

14 cups Chicken Stock, Beef Stock or
   canned chicken or beef broth
2½ cups diced carrots
2½ cups diced onions
1 tablespoon salt
2½ cups diced potaoes
2½ cups diced zucchini
2½ cups diced green beans
2½ cups cooked navy, kidney, or lima
   beans
½ cup vermicelli, broken into pieces
1 cup diced green pepper, *or* peas
   (optional)
Freshly ground black pepper
Pistou (*see* recipe below)

Put the stock or broth in a large soup pot, with carrots, onions, and salt. Bring the liquid to a boil and simmer the mixture for 45 minutes. Add all the other ingredients and cook for 25 minutes, or until the vegetables are tender. Adjust the seasonings as desired. Serve the soup in warmed bowls. The pistou should be stirred into the soup just before serving.

Pistou:

- 2 large cloves garlic, crushed
- 4 tablespoons tomato paste
- 3 tablespoons chopped fresh basil or 1½ tablespoons dried
- ⅓ cup freshly grated Parmesan cheese
- 4 tablespoons olive oil

In a small bowl combine all the ingredients except the olive oil and mix until they form a paste. Blend the oil in drop by drop, beating well after each addition. The pistou should have a mayonnaise-like consistency.

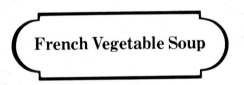

French Vegetable Soup

(4-6-servings)

- 3-4 large potatoes, sliced
- 2 tomatoes, quartered
- 2 leeks (white parts only), sliced
- 3 carrots, quartered
- 3-4 celery stalks with leaves, sliced
- 2 medium onions, sliced
- 2-3 lettuce leaves
- Bouquet garni: 1 bay leaf, ½ teaspoon dried thyme, and 4 sprigs parsley
- Salt and freshly ground black pepper
- Grated Gruyère cheese

Put all the vegetables and the bouquet garni in a large enamel or stainless steel saucepan. Add water to cover, bring the water to a boil, and simmer the mixture, covered, for 1 hour. Remove the pan from the heat and discard the bouquet garni. Purée the mixture in a food mill, blender, or food processor and season it with salt and pepper to taste. Rinse the pan, return the soup to it, and reheat it. Serve the soup in warmed bowls and sprinkle with grated cheese.

Cauliflower Soup

(8 servings)

- 1 small head cauliflower, cut into flowerets
- 4 large potatoes, cubed
- 6 cups milk
- 1 teaspoon salt
- Freshly ground white pepper
- 2 tablespoons butter
- Chopped parsley

Put the cauliflower, potatoes, milk, and salt in a large saucepan. Add pepper to taste. Bring the mixture to a boil and simmer it, covered, for 30 minutes, or until the vegetables are tender. Purée the mixture in a food mill, blender, or food processor. Rinse the pan, return the soup to it, and stir in the butter over low heat. Serve the soup in warmed bowls and sprinkle with the parsley.

Soups from the Sea

Here's a mouth-watering catch of soups made from fish and shellfish. When you buy fish, remember that the heads, bones, and trimmings are as useful as the steaks and fillets. They are the base, for example, of the White Fish Stock found in the first chapter in this section and add flavor to the Soupe de Poisson recipe in this chapter.

If your fish supply is limited to the frozen variety, try using bottled clam juice as part of the cooking liquid. It will add a full, rich flavor comparable to a stock made from fresh fish, bones, and trimmings. Be sure to reduce the amount of salt in the recipe if using clam juice.

Among the soup, chowder, and stew recipes that follow are two Mediterranean classics: Soupe de Poisson and Bouillabaisse. The Soupe de Poisson is a smooth, tomato-scented purée seasoned with a bouquet garni to which fennel and dried orange peel have been added. In French kitchens, the soup is brought to a boil, strained carefully, then brought to a boil once more for the addition of uncooked pasta. Boiled diced potatoes or even a poached egg are departures from the traditional recipe, but would be delicious additions.

Rouille, a garlicky, hot pepper sauce, is the traditional accompaniment to Soupe de Poisson. It is usually beaten into the soup, drop by drop, just before serving. However, because the spicy taste is startling to an unaccustomed palate, Rouille is best passed in a sauceboat at the table.

Proceed from the Soupe de Poisson to France's most renowned of fish soups, Bouillabaisse. The rule is—the greater the variety of fish, the greater the Bouillabaisse. Cod, flounder, haddock, sea bass, whiting, halibut, bluefish, porgy, red snapper, and sea trout are some of the finned varieties. Pieces of eel, a traditional ingredient in France, and lobster, crab, clams, mussels, and scallops are also all superb additions to a basic recipe. Serve the soup with Aioli and crusty, warm French bread to soak up every last drop. A full-bodied red or dry white wine would be appropriate, as long as it is as strong in character as the soup.

Clam Broth

New England Clam Chowder

(4-6-servings)

2 quarts littleneck clams in their shells
1 medium onion, chopped
1 stalk celery, chopped
1 carrot, chopped
4 sprigs parsley
3 cups water

Scrub the clams and put them in a soup pot with the remaining ingredients. Cook the mixture, covered, for 10 minutes or until the shells are open. Discard any clams that do not open. Serve the clams in the shells with melted butter as a sauce.

Strain the broth through a fine towel or double thickness of cheesecloth into a bowl. The broth may be served as is or reserved for a fish soup.

TOMATO-CLAM BROTH: Add 2 cups tomato juice to the strained broth. Serve hot or cold and garnish with Crème Fraîche sprinkled with chopped chives.

(4 servings)

2 ounces salt pork or 2 slices bacon, blanched for 5 minutes in boiling water and diced
1 medium onion, finely chopped
2 medium potatoes, diced
1½ cups chopped, cooked, fresh clams with their liquor or juices (*see* Note), or canned
2 cups light cream or milk
Salt and freshly grounded white pepper
Parsley
Butter
Paprika

In a skillet fry the salt pork or bacon until it is crisp. Remove it and reserve. Add the onion to the skillet and cook until it is tender.

Put the potatoes in a large saucepan, add water to cover, about 1½ cups, and bring to a boil. Simmer for about 15 minutes, or until the potatoes are just tender. Add the salt pork, onion, and clam liquor, bring the mixture to a boil, and simmer for 5 minutes. Add the cream and salt and pepper to taste. Reheat the mixture, but do not let it boil. Add clams and heat them over low heat until they are just heated through. Serve the chowder garnished with parsley and add a dab of butter sprinkled with paprika to each bowl.

NOTE: The large hardshell clams called quahogs are traditional in this New England chowder, though smaller cherrystone clams could also be used. Cook the fresh shucked clams in their liquor until they become plump. Remove the clams with a slotted spoon and finely chop them. Reserve the liquor in which they were cooked.

MANHATTAN CLAM CHOWDER: Substitute tomato juice for the cream or milk and 1½ cups clam juice for the water in which the potatoes are cooked.

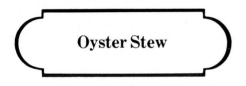

Oyster Stew

(4-6 servings)

> 3 cups shucked oysters with their liquor
> 2 cups milk
> 1 cup light cream
> Salt and freshly ground white pepper
> Butter
> Paprika

Strain the liquor from the oysters and combine it with the milk and cream in a large saucepan. Bring to a boil. Add the oysters, whole or coarsely chopped, and simmer for 1 minute, or until oysters become plump. Season with salt and pepper to taste. Serve the stew in warmed bowls with a pat of butter and a sprinkling of paprika.

Shrimp Soup

(6 servings)

> 2 tablespoons butter
> 1 onion, finely chopped
> 1 28-ounce can tomatoes
> 4 cups Chicken Stock, canned chicken broth, *or* White Fish Stock
> 1 tablespoon tomato paste
> ½ pound cooked shelled shrimp
> 1 tablespoon arrowroot, mixed with 3 tablespoons water
> Whipped cream, *or* Crème Fraîche

In a large enamel or stainless steel saucepan melt the butter and cook the onion until it is tender but not brown. Add the tomatoes and cook for 10 minutes. Stir in the stock and tomato paste and cook for 15 minutes more. Purée the mixture with the shrimp in a food mill, blender, or food processor. Return the soup to the pan, stir in the arrowroot paste, and heat, stirring until the soup is thickened. Serve the soup hot or cold and garnish with whipped cream or crème fraîche.

Soupe de Poisson (Fish Soup from the South of France)

(8 servings)

    4   tablespoons olive oil
    2   medium onions, chopped
    2   leeks, thinly sliced
    1   tablespoon all-purpose flour
    3   tomatoes, peeled, seeded and
        chopped, or ½ cup tomato purée
    2   cloves garlic, crushed
    6   pounds lean saltwater fish (such as
        cod, flounder, or haddock), with
        bones and trimmings
    12 cups water
    2   teaspoons salt
Freshly ground black pepper
Bouquet garni: 1 bay leaf, ½ teaspoon
        dried thyme, 5 sprigs parsley,
        large pinch dried fennel, and 1 strip
        dried orange rind
    2   pinches saffron
    ¼   pound vermicelli, broken into pieces
6-8 slices French bread
Freshly grated Gruyère or Parmesan
        cheese
Rouille (*see* recipe page 60)

In a large enamel or stainless steel soup pot heat the olive oil and cook the onion and leeks until they are tender but not brown. Stir in the flour and cook 1 to 2 minutes, stirring occasionally. Add the tomatoes and garlic and simmer for 15 minutes. Add the fish, water, salt, pepper to taste, bouquet garni, and saffron, and boil, uncovered, for 30 minutes. Strain the soup into a bowl, pushing it through a sieve with a wooden spoon to extract the juices. Adjust seasonings as desired. Return the soup to the pot, bring to a boil, and add the vermicelli. Boil until the pasta is tender. Toast the French bread slices and put them in soup bowls. Pour the soup over them, sprinkle with grated Gruyère or Parmesan cheese, and serve with rouille.

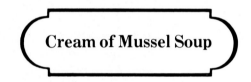

Cream of Mussel Soup

(4-6 servings)

    ¼   cup finely chopped onions
    ¼   cup finely chopped shallots
    5   sprigs parsley
    2   cups dry white wine
    1   bay leaf
    1   sprig fresh thyme or ½ teaspoon
        dried
6 tablespoons butter
Salt and freshly ground black pepper
    2   quarts mussels, well scrubbed
    2   tablespoons all-purpose flour
Pinch fresh or dried fennel
Pinch curry powder
    1   teaspoon fresh lemon juice
    2   cups scalded milk
    2   egg yolks
    1   cup heavy cream

Put the onion, shallots, parsley, wine, bay leaf, thyme, and 4 tablespoons butter in an enamel or stainless steel soup pot. Add salt and pepper to taste. Bring the liquid to a boil. Add the mussels, cover, and cook them over moderate heat for 5 to 6 minutes until the shells open. Remove the mussels, discarding any that have not opened, shell them and reserve the mussels. Reduce the cooking liquid slightly over high heat, strain it through a fine sieve, and reserve it. Melt the remaining 2 tablespoons butter in the pot and stir in the flour. Strain the broth again, stir it into the pot, and add fennel and curry powder, salt and pepper to taste, and several drops lemon juice. Adjust the seasonings as desired. Stir in enough scalded milk to obtain a creamy consistency, add the mussels, and bring to a simmer. Remove the pan from heat. In a bowl blend the egg yolks and cream with 1 cup of soup. Return the mixture to the pot, reheat the soup but do not let it boil. Serve in warmed bowls.

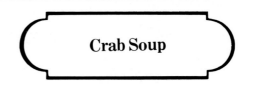

Crab Soup

(6 servings)

12	hardshell crabs or 2 cups canned crab meat
4	cups milk
1	bay leaf
1	blade mace or pinch ground mace
1	small onion, finely chopped
2	tablespoons all-purpose flour
1	cup light cream
	Salt and freshly ground white pepper
⅓	cup dry sherry

Drop the crabs into a large quantity of boiling salted water and cook them for 12 to 15 minutes until they turn bright red. Drain the crabs and remove the meat from the shells. In a large saucepan heat the milk with the bay leaf and mace for 5 minutes, strain, and reserve. In the same saucepan melt the butter and cook the onion until it is tender but not brown. Stir in the flour and cook, stirring, for 1 minute. Add the reserved milk, stirring until it is thickened. Stir in the crab meat and cream. Season with salt and pepper to taste and simmer for 15 minutes. Add the sherry and adjust the seasonings as desired. Serve the soup in warmed bowls.

Moules Marinière (Steamed Mussels)

(6-8 servings)

3 quarts mussels, well scrubbed
½ cup chopped onions
¼ cup chopped shallots
Bouquet garni: 1 bay leaf, 2 branches fresh thyme, and 5 sprigs parsley
¾ cup dry white wine
Chopped parsley

Put all ingredients in an enamel or stainless steel soup pot and cover tightly. Cook over moderate heat for about 5 to 6 minutes until the mussels open. Remove the bouquet garni and discard any mussels that have not opened. Arrange the mussels in soup bowls, ladle some broth over each, being careful not to ladle from the bottom of the pot, and serve sprinkled with parsley.

Lobster Bisque

(6 servings)

1 1-pound lobster, cooked
1½ cups Chicken Stock, canned chicken broth, *or* Vegetable Stock
1 medium onion, chopped
4 sprigs parsley
5 peppercorns
2 tablespoons butter
2 tablespoons all-purpose flour
2 cups hot milk
1 tablespoon tomato paste
½ cup heavy cream
Salt and freshly ground white pepper
Paprika

Remove all the meat from the lobster shell and chop it. Discard the green tomalley but reserve the coral, if any. Put the shell and any scraps in a large saucepan with the stock, onion, parsley, and peppercorns, bring the mixture to a boil, and simmer for 20 minutes. Strain and reserve the broth. If there is coral, push it through a fine sieve and combine it with the butter and flour to make a paste. (If there is no coral, combine the butter and flour.) Add the mixture to the hot milk, stir until it is thickened, and add it to the reserved broth. Stir in the tomato paste and add the lobster meat and cream. Season with salt and pepper to taste and heat through. Sprinkle with paprika and serve.

Bouillabaisse

(6-8 servings)

8 pounds various lean saltwater fish (such as sea bass, red snapper, cod, flounder, haddock) and shellfish (such as lobster, crab, shrimp, mussels, clams) to make a combination of 6 to 8 different varieties
1 recipe Soupe de Poisson, without vermicelli
Rouille or Aioli (*see* recipes below)

Clean all the fish and shellfish. Cut fish and larger shellfish and shrimp into 2-inch pieces. Mussels and clams can be left in their shells. In an enamel or stainless steel soup pot bring the soupe de poisson to a boil and add the shellfish and firm-fleshed fish, a few pieces at a time, so that the liquid maintains a boil. Boil for 5 minutes. Add the tender-fleshed fish and boil for 5 minutes more. The soup is ready as soon as the fish flakes easily and the clams or mussels, if any, have opened. Serve in large soup plates with rouille or aioli.

Rouille:
2 hot red peppers, fresh or canned
1 sweet red pepper, chopped, or a 4-ounce jar pimientos
6 cloves garlic, crushed
1½ cups fresh bread crumbs
8 tablespoons Soupe de Poisson
6 fresh basil leaves, chopped
Salt and freshly ground black pepper
8 tablespoons olive oil

If using fresh peppers, simmer them in salted water to cover until tender. Using a food processor, blender, or mortar and pestle, combine all ingredients, except the oil, to form a paste. Add the oil drop by drop (add more soup if necessary) until the paste has the consistency of mayonnaise.

NOTE: In France, Rouille is the traditional accompaniment to Soupe de Poisson. Rouille means "rust" in French, and this sauce gets its name from its color. It is *very hot*. Add to the soup with caution.

Aioli:
5 cloves garlic, or to taste, mashed to a paste
1 egg yolk
1 cup olive oil
1 tablespoon fresh lemon juice
1 tablespoon cold water
Pinch salt

In a small bowl combine the garlic and egg yolk, then add the oil drop by drop, using a whisk to blend vigorously. As with mayonnaise, be sure to blend well after each addition. Add lemon juice, water, and salt and blend.

NOTE: Aioli can also be easily made in a blender or food processor.

Stella Standard's Red Snapper Chowder

(4-6 servings)

Fish Stock:
Red snapper trimmings, including the bones and head, but not gills
1 cup water
2 cups bottled clam juice
1 cup dry white wine or dry vermouth
1 onion, thinly sliced
1 carrot, thinly sliced
1 stalk celery, sliced
1 teaspoon dried thyme
1 leek, sliced
1 clove garlic, crushed
Salt and freshly ground white pepper

The chowder:
2 slices salt pork, diced
2½ pounds red snapper fillets
2 cups diced onions
2 cups cubed potatoes
Salt and freshly ground white pepper
½ cup cracker crumbs
1 cup heavy cream
2 egg yolks

In an enamel or stainless steel soup pot make the stock with all ingredients. Cook, covered, for 25 minutes, strain, and set aside. In a heavy deep skillet lightly cook the salt pork. On it alternate layers of fish, onions, potatoes, and cracker crumbs, lightly seasoning each layer with salt and pepper to taste. Pour in the stock and cook, covered, very slowly for 40 minutes. Scald the cream, mix with the egg yolks, and pour over the chowder. Serve in warmed soup bowls.

Hearty Soups

Take a tip from country cooks the world over and serve supper in a soup tureen. Choose any one of these hearty soups from an international melange — an Indian Mulligatawny flavored with a hint of curry powder; Avgolemono, the egg and lemon soup of Greece; Cock-a-Leekie, a Scotch Broth from the British Isles. These hearty soups make satisfying meals with little more than some fragrant slices of warm bread, a pat or two of butter, and a crisp salad tossed with a lemon juice dressing.

Minestrone is Italy's contribution — a thick and nourishing blend of vegetables and herbs, richly colored with plum tomatoes. Ingredients and appearance vary from one area to another, depending on the kinds and colors of beans and the pasta shapes that are traditional. In most minestrones the pasta is in the form of tiny tubes, shells, or elbows, but rice is used in Milan. The Genoese-style soup features potatoes, shreds of spinach, and a sprinkling of bacon. Whatever the combination of ingredients, a good minestrone should be served with freshly grated Parmesan cheese as a garnish.

Borscht, the traditional beet and cabbage soup of Russia, Poland, and the Ukraine, is an international favorite. Its texture can vary from a smooth purée to "Moscow borscht," filled with chunks of carrots, potatoes, parsnips, cabbage, onion, and, of course, plenty of chopped beets. Whether it's smooth or chunky, served hot or cold, you'll know a borscht by its color — the deep, ruby red of the beetroot. To achieve and retain the glowing color, some cooks simmer the meat, vegetables, and seasonings with only half the beet juice called for in the recipe and stir in the remaining juice just before serving, taking care that the soup does not boil after that addition or the jewel-like color will fade.

Borscht refrigerates and freezes well, but after reheating the color will need to be revitalized. Just grate a peeled, raw beet into half a cup of cold water or chilled red wine, and add to the soup before serving.

From south of the border comes Gallina Pinta, a thick peasant soup-stew of oxtail, pork, whole hominy, and beans. No one seems to know how it got its name, which means, literally, "speckled hen."

For a touch of balmy climes — the Caribbean, in particular — add a clove or two and a pinch of cumin to Black Bean Soup. Garnish it as they do in Cuba with big spoonfuls of hot, cooked white rice.

Black Bean Soup

(8 servings)

1 cup dried black beans, soaked overnight in 2 cups water, drained
4 cups water
1 small onion, chopped
1 clove garlic
1 stalk celery, chopped
1 carrot, chopped
1 branch fresh thyme or ¼ teaspoon dried
1 bay leaf
4 sprigs parsley
Salt
Freshly ground black pepper
Juice of 1 lemon
1 tablespoon butter, softened
1 tablespoon all-purpose flour
½ cup dry sherry
2 hard-boiled eggs, sliced
1 lemon, thinly sliced

Put the black beans in a large saucepan and add the water, onion, garlic, celery, carrot, and herbs. Bring the liquid to a boil over moderate heat and simmer, partially covered, for 3 to 4 hours, until the beans are very tender. Add water as needed. Remove the bay leaf and thyme branch, if used, and purée the mixture in a food mill, blender, or food processor. Add lemon juice, season with salt and pepper to taste, and return the soup to the pan. Make a paste of the butter and flour, stir it into the soup and cook the soup, stirring, for a few minutes. Just before serving, add the sherry. Garnish each bowl with a slice of egg and lemon.

Poule au Pot (Chicken in the Pot)

(4 servings)

1 3-pound chicken
6 cups Chicken Stock or chicken bouillon made from 6 cubes with 6 cups water
3 Sweet Italian sausages, cut into 1-inch pieces
Bouquet garni: 1 bay leaf, ½ teaspoon dried thyme, and 3 sprigs parsley
4 small white turnips, quartered and cut into 1½-inch pieces
2 stalks celery, split lengthwise and cut into 1½-inch pieces
4 carrots, quartered lengthwise and cut into 1½-inch pieces
2 zucchini, quartered lengthwise and cut into 1½-inch pieces
1 cup quartered leeks or scallions (white part only)
¼ cup uncooked rice
Salt and freshly ground black pepper

Truss the chicken, put it into a soup pot just large enough to hold all the ingredients, and cover it with water. Bring the water to a boil and drain the liquid, leaving the chicken in the pot. Add the stock or bouillon, sausage, bouquet garni, and all the vegetables, except the zucchini and the leeks or scallions. Bring the mixture to a boil and simmer it for 20 minutes. Add the zucchini and leeks or scallions and cook for 5 minutes. Add the rice and salt and pepper to taste and cook until the rice and vegetables are tender, for about 15 to 20 minutes. Remove the chicken, remove the trussing strings, and carve the chicken into serving pieces. Arrange a piece of chicken and some rice and vegetables in each deep soup bowl and pour some stock over them.

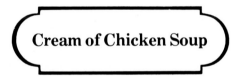

Cream of Chicken Soup

(6 servings)

- 3 tablespoons butter
- 3 tablespoons all-purpose flour
- 4 cups Chicken Stock or canned chicken broth
- 1 cup light cream
- 2 egg yolks
- ¼ cup Madeira wine or dry sherry
- Salt and freshly ground white pepper
- Paprika

In a large saucepan melt the butter, stir in the flour, and cook for 1 minute. Stir in the stock or broth and stir until the mixture is thickened. Add ¾ of the cream, bring to a boil, and remove the pan from the heat. In a small bowl beat the egg yolks with the remaining ¼ cup cream and wine or sherry. Slowly beat in some of the hot liquid. Then beat the egg-wine mixture into the soup. Reheat but do not let the soup boil or the eggs will scramble. Season the soup with salt and pepper to taste and sprinkle with paprika.

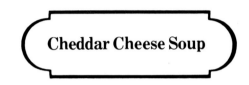

Cheddar Cheese Soup

(6 servings)

- 4 tablespoons butter
- 1 medium onion, finely chopped
- ¼ cup all-purpose flour
- 3 cups Chicken Stock or canned chicken broth
- 3 cups milk
- 4 cups coarsely grated mild Cheddar cheese

In a large saucepan melt the butter and cook the onion until it is tender, for about 5 minutes. Stir in the flour and cook, stirring, until it is blended. Add the stock or broth gradually and cook, stirring constantly, until it is thickened. Stir in the milk, bring the mixture to a boil, and remove the pan from heat. Add the cheese, stirring until it melts. If the cheese does not melt completely, cook the soup over low heat for 1 to 2 minutes. Serve the soup immediately.

Avgolemono (Greek Egg & Lemon Soup)

(6-8 servings)

2 tablespoons butter
2 shallots, minced
2 tablespoons all-purpose flour
6 cups Chicken Stock or canned chicken broth
Juice of ½ lemon, or to taste
Zest of 1 lemon
3 egg yolks
Salt and freshly ground white pepper
⅓ cup heavy cream, whipped

In a large enamel or stainless steel saucepan melt the butter and cook the shallots for 2 to 3 minutes, or until they are tender but not brown. Remove the pan from the heat and stir in the flour. Over heat add the stock or broth and bring the mixture to a boil, stirring constantly. Add the lemon juice and zest and simmer for 15 to 20 minutes. Strain the soup. Rinse the pan and return the soup to it. In a small bowl beat the egg yolks slightly and beat in 1 cup warm soup. Then add the yolk mixture to the soup, season it with salt and pepper to taste, and reheat it but do not let it boil. Garnish with dollops of whipped cream and serve.

Cock-a-Leekie

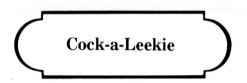

(8-10 servings)

1 5-6 pound chicken
10 cups water
Salt and freshly ground black pepper
8 large leeks (white parts only), sliced
2 tablespoons uncooked rice
Chopped parsley

Put the chicken in a large soup pot, add the water, and season with salt and pepper. Bring the water to a boil and skim the surface. Simmer, covered, for 1 hour. Skim the fat and add the leeks and rice. Cook for 1 hour, or until chicken is tender, and remove the chicken from the pot. Let the chicken cool slightly, remove the meat from the bones, cut it into small strips, and reserve it. Skim any remaining fat from the stock. Adjust seasonings as desired. Garnish with strips of chicken, sprinkle with the parsley, and serve.

Split Pea Soup

(4-6 servings)

2 cups split peas
10 cups Chicken Stock, canned chicken broth, *or* water
1 carrot, sliced
1 stalk celery, chopped
1 medium onion, sliced
1 clove garlic
1 cup chopped lettuce or spinach
Bouquet garni: 1 bay leaf, ½ teaspoon dried thyme, and 4 sprigs parsley
Salt and freshly ground black pepper
Croutons

In a soup pot combine the split peas, stock, broth, or water, carrot, celery, onion, garlic, lettuce or spinach, and bouquet garni. Bring the liquid to a boil, and simmer it, partially covered, adding more stock or water as needed, for 2 to 3 hours, or until the peas are tender. Stir occasionally to prevent scorching. Remove the bouquet garni, and purée the mixture in a food mill, blender, or food processor. Rinse the pot, return the soup to it, and season with salt and pepper to taste. Add more stock or water if the soup is too thick. Serve the soup with croutons.

WITH FRANKFURTERS: Add slices of cooked frankfurters to the soup before serving. (Other kinds of sausage can be used.)

WITH HAM: Toss cubes of cooked ham in butter in a skillet until they are heated through and add them to soup before serving.

Mrs. Janedis' Lentil Soup

(6 servings)

2 carrots, thinly sliced
2 cups lentils, rinsed
8 cups water
2 medium onions, chopped
2 stalks celery, chopped
2 teaspoons salt
Freshly ground black pepper
1 bay leaf
1 clove garlic, crushed
1 tablespoon or more olive oil
½ cup tomato sauce

Blanch the carrots in boiling water for 5 minutes, drain, and reserve them. Put the lentils in an enamel or stainless steel soup pot, add the water, and bring to a boil. Add the onions, celery, salt, pepper to taste, the bay leaf, and garlic. Simmer the mixture until the lentils are tender, for 1 to 1½ hours. Adjust the seasonings as desired. Add the carrots, oil to taste, and tomato sauce and cook until the carrots are heated through. Before serving, remove the bay leaf.

Meatball Soup

Minestrone

(6 servings)

- 1 pound lean ground beef
- ½ pound lean ground pork
- ⅓ cup uncooked rice
- 2 eggs
- 1 large onion, grated
- 3 tablespoons finely chopped parsley

Salt and freshly ground black pepper

- 8 cups Beef Stock, canned beef broth, *or* Vegetable Stock
- ½ cup plain yogurt

In a bowl combine the meats, rice, 1 egg, onion, 2 tablespoons parsley, and salt and pepper to taste. Bring the stock or broth to a boil in a large saucepan. Shape the meat mixture into 1-inch balls and drop them, 1 at a time, into the stock. Simmer for about 40 minutes, or until rice in a meatball tastes tender when tested. Beat the yogurt together with the remaining egg and just before serving pour the mixture into a soup tureen. Add the soup a little at a time, stirring so that the egg does not scramble. Sprinkle the soup with the remaining tablespoon of parsley.

(4 servings)

- 1 cup sliced onions
- ⅓ cup olive oil
- 2 carrots, diced
- 2 stalks celery, diced
- 2 zucchini, diced
- 1 cup shredded cabbage
- ½ cup chopped canned Italian plum tomatoes, with their juice
- ½ teaspoon dried basil

Salt and freshly ground black pepper

- 1 cup Chicken Stock, Beef Stock, or canned chicken or beef broth
- 1 cup water
- 1 cup canned drained white beans (cannellini)

Freshly grated Parmesan cheese

In a soup pot heat the oil and cook the onions until they are golden. Stir in all the diced vegetables and cabbage and add the tomatoes and their juice, basil, and salt and pepper to taste. Stir in stock or broth and water. If the liquid does not cover the vegetables, add more water. Bring the liquid to a boil and simmer it very gently for 2 hours. Add the beans the last 10 minutes of cooking. Adjust the seasonings as desired and serve the minestrone with Parmesan cheese.

Mulligatawny

(6 servings)

- 1 pound lean breast of lamb
- 2 tablespoons oil
- 2 medium onions, sliced
- 1 carrot, sliced
- 1 firm, tart apple, cored and sliced
- 1 tablespoon curry powder
- 6 tablespoons all-purpose flour
- 6 cups Chicken Stock, canned chicken broth, *or* water
- 1 cup milk
- 1 teaspoon arrowroot, mixed with 1 tablespoon water (optional)

Salt and freshly ground black pepper
Fresh lemon juice

In a soup pot heat the oil, add the lamb, and cook it until it is brown. Remove the meat and add the onions, carrot, and apple. Cook the mixture for 3 minutes, add the curry powder, and cook for 2 minutes. Stir in the flour and cook for 1 minute. Add the stock, broth, or water, bring the liquid to a boil, and return the meat to pot. Cover and simmer for 1½ hours. Remove the meat, cut it into thin strips, and reserve it, discarding the bones. Purée the vegetables in a food mill, blender, or food processor. Rinse the pot, return the soup to it, and add the milk. Bring the soup to a boil. (If it is not as thick as desired, stir in the arrowroot paste and heat until the soup thickens.) Season with salt, pepper, and lemon juice to taste and serve the soup with the strips of lamb.

Diana Kennedy's Gallina Pinta

(6-8 servings)

- 1 oxtail (about 1½-2 pounds), trimmed of most, but not all fat, and cut into small pieces
- ½ onion, thickly sliced
- 2 cloves garlic
- 2 teaspoons salt
- ½ cup dried pinto beans
- 6 peppercorns
- 8 cups water
- 1 pound country-style pork spareribs, cut into small pieces
- 1 1-pound can whole hominy, drained
  Salt

In a large saucepan put the oxtail, onion, garlic, salt, pinto beans, and peppercorns, cover with water, and bring to a boil. Simmer the mixture for 1 hour. Add the spareribs and hominy and cook, uncovered, for 1 to 1½ hours, until the meat is very tender and the beans are soft. Add salt to taste and serve in warmed deep bowls with tortillas.

Pot-au-Feu (Boiled Beef with Vegetables)

(6 servings)

- 2 pounds short ribs of beef or plate of beef
- 2 pounds rump or round of beef
- 1 pound veal bones, preferably the knuckle, sawed into 3 pieces
- 16 cups water
- 2 teaspoons salt
- 4 carrots, halved lengthwise
- 4 medium onions, 1 studded with 3 cloves
- 2 stalks celery
- 3 leeks (white parts only), cut into 1½-inch pieces
- 6 small white turnips
- Freshly ground black pepper
- Bouquet garni: 1 bay leaf, 1 teaspoon dried thyme, and 5 sprigs parsley

Put the meat and bones in a large soup pot with the water and salt, bring the liquid to a boil, uncovered, over low heat, and simmer the mixture, skimming the froth from the surface, for 1 hour. Add the vegetables, pepper to taste, and bouquet garni. Simmer the soup for 2½ to 3 hours, until meat is tender. Remove the bones and discard them. Arrange the meat and vegetables on a platter and serve with bowls of the stock.

NOTE: A small chicken, cut into serving pieces, may be substituted for 1 pound of the beef. Add it to the pot along with the vegetables.

Scotch Broth

(10 servings)

- 2½ pounds lamb shanks, shoulder, neck, or rib with bones, cut into 2-inch pieces
- 10 cups water
- ½ cup pearl barley
- 3 tablespoons butter
- 2 carrots, diced
- 2 medium onions, coarsely chopped
- ½ cup diced yellow turnip
- 2 stalks celery
- Salt and freshly ground black pepper

Put the lamb in a large soup pot, add the water and barley, and bring the mixture to a boil. Simmer, covered, for 2 hours, or until the meat is tender. Remove the bones and meat, then chop the meat and reserve.

In a skillet melt the butter and cook the vegetables very slowly for 15 minutes. Add the meat and vegetables to the soup and cook the mixture for 30 minutes more. Season with salt and pepper to taste, and serve.

Richard Sax's Hungarian Gulyás Soup

(8 servings)

3 tablespoons lard, *or* vegetable oil
2 onions, halved and thickly sliced
2 cloves garlic, minced
2 sweet red peppers, cut into 1-inch squares
4 carrots, thickly sliced
3 stalks celery, thickly sliced
1 small turnip, peeled, diced (optional)
¼ cup Hungarian paprika, preferably medium-hot
2-3 tomatoes, peeled, seeded, and diced
4 cups Beef Stock or canned beef broth
4 medium potatoes, diced
1½ cups (approximately) cooked pot roast, boiled beef, or roast beef, diced
2 teaspoons salt
½ teaspoon freshly ground black pepper
Pinch of dried thyme or marjoram
1 cup green beans, trimmed and cut into 1-inch lengths
1 cup mushrooms, thickly sliced
1½ cups sour cream
Chopped parsley

In a large flameproof casserole heat the lard or oil until hot, add the onions, and cook them for about 6 minutes, or until they are slightly wilted. Add the garlic, peppers, carrots, celery, and turnip, if desired, and toss to coat the vegetables with fat. Cook over moderate heat for 6 to 8 minutes, or until the vegetables begin to soften. Stir in the paprika and cook for 3 minutes. Add the tomatoes, stir, and cook for about 2 minutes, or until they begin to give up their liquid. Add the stock or broth, potatoes, meat, salt, black pepper, and thyme or marjoram to taste. Bring the soup to a boil and simmer it, partially covered, for 30 minutes, or until the ingredients are just tender. Do not overcook.

Remove about 1 cup of the solid vegetables and purée them in a food mill, blender, or food processor with a little of the liquid until they are almost smooth. Return the purée to the soup and stir to thicken. (If you wish to have a thicker soup, purée another cup or so of the solids as above.) Add the green beans to the soup and simmer for 5 minutes. Add the mushrooms and simmer for 3 minutes. Adjust the seasonings, adding salt and pepper if needed.

Stir half of the sour cream into the soup. Ladle the soup into bowls and garnish each serving with a spoonful of sour cream topped with chopped parsley.

Chicken Soup with Mushrooms

(6-8 servings)

- 1   4-5 pound chicken
- 2   medium onions, quartered
- 2   carrots, quartered
- ¾ cup chopped celery
- Bouquet garni: 1 bay leaf, ¼ teaspoon dried thyme, and 5 sprigs parsley
- Salt and freshly ground black pepper
- 1   tablespoon butter
- 2   teaspoons fresh lemon juice
- ¼ pound mushrooms, thinly sliced

In a soup pot combine the chicken, onions, carrots, celery, and bouquet garni and add water to cover. Bring the liquid to a boil, skim the surface, and simmer the mixture, covered, until the chicken and vegetables are tender. Remove the chicken, remove the meat from the bones, and reserve it. Return the bones to the pot and cook them for 2 hours more, adding water as needed. Strain the stock into a bowl and add salt and pepper to taste.

In a small skillet melt the butter, add the lemon juice and mushrooms, and cook them for 2 minutes. Serve the stock garnished with the mushrooms and strips of white meat of chicken.

The Russian Tea Room's Hot Borscht

(8 servings)

- ¾ cup finely chopped carrots
- 1½ cups finely chopped onions
- 1½ cups finely chopped celery
- 1½ parsnips, finely chopped
- 4   medium beets, cooked, and finely chopped
- 2   tablespoons butter
- 3   cups Beef Stock, canned beef broth, *or* Vegetable Stock
- 1½ cups finely shredded cabbage
- 1½ cups peeled, seeded tomatoes or drained canned tomatoes, chopped
- Salt and freshly ground black pepper
- Sour cream
- Snipped fresh dill

In a soup pot barely cover the carrots, onions, celery, and parsnips with boiling water and boil them gently, covered, for 20 minutes. Add the beets, butter, stock or broth, cabbage, tomatoes, and salt and pepper to taste and boil for 15 minutes more. Serve the borscht hot and garnish it with sour cream and dill.

Summer Soups

Cooled soups—chilled soups—iced soups. Ladle them into soup bowls, pour them into chilled thermos bottles to take to picnics, offer them on the rocks at cocktail time.

If you plan to serve a soup cold, remember that cooked foods lose their flavor as they chill. Extra seasonings should be added as the soup cooks and it should be tasted for seasoning after it has been refrigerated. You may wish to add a dash of lemon juice, a sprinkling of salt and pepper, or a pinch or two of fresh, minced herbs.

Many of the soups in this chapter can be served warm. But be careful—a creamed summer soup tastes better warm than piping hot. An easy way to achieve the correct serving temperature is to remove the simmering soup from the heat and ladle a small amount into the cream or milk called for in the recipe. Blend the liquids and then gently stir the mixture into the soup. The cooler liquid should bring the temperature down.

For delicately colored, puréed soups, such as Crème d'Avocat, Cold Minted Pea Soup, Carrot Vichyssoise, and Purée de Cresson (Watercress Soup), you might try an easy and attractive garnish. Pour the soup into individual bowls, then swirl in some cream to create a marbled pattern.

For a garden party serve unusual and colorful cherry or blueberry soup from northern Europe. For a truly beautiful effect serve the soup in a glass bowl set in a dish of cracked ice.

Less familiar, but intriguing, is Chlodnik. This special version of a traditional Polish summertime treat is a rose-colored beet and shrimp soup strewn with chopped cucumbers, ham, and dill. A hearty Chlodnik starts with a base of chicken stock. The greens include radishes and scallions and can be varied with beet tops, sorrel, or chives. Sour cream or buttermilk stirred into the chilled soup adds a tangy flavor. Garnishes also vary: slices of lemon and hard-boiled egg, diced fresh cucumber, cooked beets, whole shrimp, or even a slice of sour pickle. In many areas of Poland, Chlodnik is poured over a cube of ice in each bowl and then served.

Cream of Asparagus Soup

(8-10 servings)

1½ pounds asparagus, woody ends removed
8 cups Chicken Stock, canned chicken broth, *or* Vegetable Stock
1 medium onion, diced
4 sprigs parsley
¼ cup butter
¼ cup all-purpose flour
½ cup heavy cream
Salt and freshly ground white pepper

Cut the tips from the asparagus and cook them in boiling water in an enamel or stainless steel pot until tender. Set them aside. Cut the rest of the asparagus into 2-inch pieces and put it in a large saucepan with the stock or broth, onion, and parsley. Cook until tender. Purée the mixture in a food mill, blender, or food processor. Rinse the pan and melt the butter in it. Stir in flour and cook, stirring, for 1 minute. Add the stock and cream and stir until mixture is thickened. Adjust the seasonings as desired. Just before serving, add asparagus tips.

Cream of Celery Soup

(4 servings)

2 cups finely chopped celery
1 medium onion, minced
2 tablespoons butter
2 tablespoons all-purpose flour
2 cups Chicken Stock or canned chicken broth
1½ cups light cream
½ teaspoon grated nutmeg
Salt and freshly ground white pepper
Cucumber slices

In a large saucepan melt the butter and cook the celery and onion until they are transparent. Sprinkle with flour and cook for 1 minute more. Stir in the stock or broth and cream and stir until the mixture is thickened. Add the nutmeg and salt and pepper to taste. Cook, stirring, for 5 minutes. Chill the soup and serve it with cucumber slices as a garnish.

Crème d'Avocat
(Cream of Avocado Soup)

(6 servings)

2 tablespoons butter
½ cup minced onion
2 tablespoons all-purpose flour
3 cups Chicken Stock or canned chicken broth
1 tablespoon fresh lemon juice
1 tablespoon drained prepared horseradish
1 tablespoon tarragon vinegar
1 clove garlic, crushed
½ teaspoon salt
¼ teaspoon curry powder
¼ teaspoon dried tarragon
Freshly ground black pepper
1 ripe avocado
1 cup milk
1 cup light cream

In a large saucepan melt the butter and cook the onion until it is transparent. Add the flour and stir until smooth. Stir in half the stock or broth, stirring constantly until it boils and thickens. Add the lemon juice, horseradish, vinegar, garlic, salt, curry powder, tarragon, and pepper to taste and simmer, covered, for 10 minutes. Purée the mixture in a food mill, blender, or food processor and return it to the pan. Peel the avocado with a stainless steel knife to prevent darkening and purée it with the remaining stock or broth. Add the purée to the pan and stir in the milk and cream. Cook, stirring, until the soup is heated through. Serve the soup hot or cold in glass bowls.

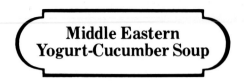

Middle Eastern Yogurt-Cucumber Soup

(4 servings)

½ cup raisins, soaked in ½ cup warm water
2 cups plain yogurt
1 large cucumber, peeled, seeded, and grated
1 small onion, grated
1 clove garlic, crushed (optional)
1½ teaspoons salt
¼ teaspoon freshly ground black pepper
2 cups milk
½ cup sour cream (optional)
2 teaspoons chopped fresh dill or ½ teaspoon dried
Cucumber slices

In a large bowl or saucepan combine all ingredients except the cucumber slices. Be sure to include the water in which the raisins have soaked. Chill the soup for at least 3 hours. Serve in chilled bowls and garnish with the cucumber slices.

Cucumber Soup

(6 servings)

2 shallots, chopped
1 small onion, chopped
1 tablespoon butter
½ teaspoon dried thyme
½ cup chopped parsley
½ cup finely chopped celery
3 potatoes, quartered
1 teaspoon salt
3 cups Chicken Stock or canned chicken broth
1 large cucumber, peeled, seeded, and grated or puréed
2 cups sour cream, *or* 1 cup milk
2 drops hot pepper sauce
½ teaspoon dried dill
Chopped fresh dill or parsley

In a large saucepan melt the butter and cook the shallots and onion until they are tender but not brown. Add the thyme, parsley, celery, potatoes, salt, and stock or broth and cook, covered, over low heat until the potatoes are tender. Purée the mixture in a food mill, blender, or food processor and chill it in a serving bowl. Before serving, add the cucumber, sour cream or milk, hot pepper sauce, and dill, and sprinkle with dill or parsley.

Vichyssoise (Cold Leek & Potato Soup)

(8 servings)

- 2 tablespoons butter
- 5 leeks (white parts only), sliced
- 1 medium onion, sliced
- 4 potatoes, sliced
- Salt and freshly ground white pepper
- 4 cups Chicken Stock or canned chicken broth
- 2 cups milk
- 2½ cups light cream
- Chopped fresh chives

In a large saucepan melt the butter and cook the leeks and onion 5 minutes until they are tender but not brown. Add the potatoes, salt and pepper to taste and the stock or broth. Bring the liquid to a boil and simmer it 20 minutes until the vegetables are tender. Purée the mixture in a food mill, blender, or food processor and return it to the pan. Stir in the milk and half the cream and bring to a boil. Adjust the seasonings as desired. Chill the soup and just before serving add the remaining cream. Sprinkle with chives.

Gazpacho

(6 servings)

- 2 cups tomato juice
- 1 cup tomatoes, peeled, seeded, and finely chopped
- ½ cup finely chopped green pepper
- ½ cup finely chopped peeled cucumber
- ½ cup finely chopped celery
- ¼ cup minced onion
- 1 tablespoon chopped parsley
- 1 teaspoon chopped fresh chives
- 1 small clove garlic, crushed
- 1 tablespoon tarragon vinegar
- 1 tablespoon olive oil
- ½ teaspoon salt
- ¼ teaspoon freshly ground black pepper
- Croutons

In a large bowl combine all ingredients except the croutons and chill the soup for at least 4 hours. If you prefer a smooth soup, purée the mixture in a food mill, blender, or food processor for 10 seconds before chilling. Reserve some chopped tomato, cucumber, pepper, and celery as garnishes. Transfer the soup to a chilled tureen and garnish with croutons before serving.

Minted Pea Soup

(4 servings)

2 cups green peas, fresh or frozen
1 small onion, thinly sliced
1 cup water
2 tablespoons all-purpose flour
3 cups Chicken Stock or canned chicken broth
½ cup heavy cream
Salt and freshly ground black pepper
Finely chopped fresh mint

Cook the peas and onion in the water until they are tender. In a large saucepan whisk together the flour and ½ cup of the stock or broth until smooth. Add the remaining stock and cook, stirring until it is thickened. Purée the peas and onions with the water in which they were cooked in a food mill, blender, or food processor and add the purée to the stock. Bring to a boil, add the cream, and season with salt and pepper to taste. Chill the soup and serve it with mint. If soup is too thick, stir in more cream.

Swedish Fruit Soup

(4-6 servings)

¼ pound dried apples or peaches
¼ pound dried apricots
¼ pound dried, pitted prunes
4 cups water
½ cup sugar
Juice of 1 lemon
½ cinnamon stick
1 tablespoon arrowroot, mixed with 3 tablespoons water
Heavy cream

In an enamel or stainless steel saucepan soak the fruit in the water for 1½ hours. Add the sugar, lemon juice, and cinnamon stick, bring the liquid to a boil, and simmer it until the fruit is tender, for 15 to 20 minutes. Stir in the arrowroot paste and heat until the soup is thickened, for about 1 minute. Chill the soup. Remove the cinnamon stick and serve with a pitcher of cream.

Zucchini Soup

(8 servings)

8 cups Chicken Stock or canned chicken broth
1 onion, thinly sliced
Pinch chervil, fresh or dried
Pinch oregano, fresh or dried
Salt and freshly ground black pepper
4-5 small unpeeled zucchini, cut into 1-inch pieces
½ cup green peas, fresh or frozen
Sour cream
Finely chopped fresh chervil or oregano

In a soup pot put the stock or broth, onion, and herbs, season with salt and pepper to taste, and bring the liquid to a boil. Add the zucchini and peas and simmer for 20 minutes, or until the vegetables are tender. Purée the mixture in a food mill, blender, or food processor, return it to the pot, and reheat. Serve the soup with sour cream and sprinkle with chervil or oregano.

Carrot Vichyssoise

(4-6 servings)

2 cups diced potatoes
1¼ cups sliced carrots
1 leek (white part only), sliced
3 cups Chicken Stock or canned chicken broth
1 cup heavy cream
Salt and freshly ground white pepper
Shredded raw carrot

In a large saucepan combine the potatoes, carrots, leek, and stock or broth. Bring the liquid to a boil and simmer the mixture, partially covered, for 25 minutes, or until the vegetables are tender. Purée the mixture in a food mill, blender, or food processor. Transfer the soup to a bowl, stir in the cream, and add salt and pepper to taste. Chill the soup and serve it in chilled bowls. Garnish with carrot shreds.

(Preceding pages) Purée de cresson, zucchini soup, carrot vichysoisse

Purée de Cresson
(Watercress Soup)

(4 servings)

1 bunch watercress, tough stems
   removed (reserve 1 sprig for garnish)
1 tablespoon butter
1 large potato, diced
1 scallion, sliced
4 sprigs parsley
3 cups Chicken Stock or canned chicken
   broth
Salt and freshly ground black pepper
1 egg yolk
1 tablespoon fresh lemon juice
¼ cup heavy cream

In a small skillet melt the butter, add the watercress, and cook until it is wilted. Put the potato, scallion, parsley, and stock or broth in a saucepan, bring the liquid to a boil, and simmer it for 20 minutes, until the potato is tender. Add the watercress. Purée the mixture in a food mill, blender, or food processor and return it to the pan. Just before serving, bring the soup to a simmer and season it with salt and pepper to taste. In a small bowl whisk together the egg yolk, lemon juice, cream, and a few spoonfuls of hot soup. Pour into the soup and reheat the mixture but do not let it boil. Serve the soup in a warmed tureen. Garnish with the reserved sprig of watercress.

To serve cold, chill the mixture and add more cream or milk if soup is too thick. Adjust the seasonings as desired.

Cherry Soup

(4-6 servings)

- 1   pound pitted Bing cherries
- 2½   cups water
- ½   cup dry red wine
- ½   cup fresh orange juice
- 4   tablespoons sugar
- 1   teaspoon arrowroot, mixed with 1 tablespoon water
- ½   cup heavy cream, whipped
- Ground cinnamon

In an enamel or stainless steel saucepan combine the cherries, water, wine, orange juice, and sugar and cook for about 10 minutes, until the cherries are tender. Purée the mixture in a food mill, blender, or food processor and return it to the pan. Stir in the arrowroot paste and heat until the soup is thickened, for about 1 minute. Chill the soup and serve it with whipped cream and a sprinkling of cinnamon.

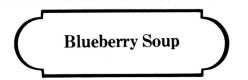

Blueberry Soup

(6 servings)

- 4   cups water
- 3   cups blueberries
- 3   tablespoons or more sugar
- 2   tablespoons arrowroot, mixed with 6 tablespoons water
- ½   cup heavy cream, whipped

In a saucepan bring the water to a boil and add the sugar and fruit. Simmer for 3 minutes, or until fruit is tender. Stir in the arrowroot paste and heat until the soup is thickened, for about 1 minute. Add more sugar if desired. Chill the soup and serve with dollops of whipped cream.

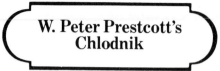

W. Peter Prestcott's Chlodnik

(8 servings)

1 bunch beets, trimmed, scrubbed, but unpeeled
4 cups Chicken Stock or canned chicken broth
2 cucumbers, peeled, seeded, and chopped
6 radishes, thinly sliced
6 scallions, finely chopped
1 tablespoon red-wine vinegar
3 tablespoons chopped fresh dill
1 cup chopped cooked ham
1 cup chopped cooked shrimp
Salt and freshly ground black pepper
Sour cream or buttermilk
2 hard-boiled eggs, chopped
Sprigs fresh dill

In a large saucepan bring the beets to a boil in the stock or broth and cook them slowly for about 40 minutes, or until they are tender. Remove the beets and reserve the stock.

Peel the beets, cut them into julienne strips, and add them to the stock with the remaining ingredients. Season with salt and pepper to taste. Chill the soup, covered, overnight if possible. Swirl sour cream or buttermilk into each bowl and garnish with chopped egg and dill.

Tomato Soup

(4 servings)

4 cups water
½ pound potatoes, chopped
½ pound tomatoes, peeled, seeded, and chopped
1 medium onion, chopped
1 bay leaf
½ teaspoon dried thyme
Salt and freshly ground black pepper
Butter

Put all the ingredients except the butter in a large enamel or stainless steel saucepan, bring the mixture to a boil, and simmer it for 15 to 20 minutes, or until the vegetables are tender. Remove the bay leaf. Purée the mixture in a food mill, blender, or food processor. Rinse the pan and return the soup to it. Reheat it. Serve in warmed bowls and top each serving with a small pat of butter.

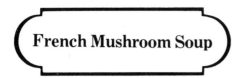

French Mushroom Soup

(4 servings)

- 4 tablespoons butter
- 4 tablespoons all-purpose flour
- 4 cups Chicken Stock or canned chicken broth
- ¼ pound mushrooms (rinsed in white vinegar to retard discoloring), chopped

Salt and freshly ground white pepper

- 4 slices stale French bread
- 4 tablespoons grated Gruyère cheese

In a large saucepan melt the butter, add the flour, and stir the mixture over low heat for 1 minute. Add the stock or broth and stir until mixture is thickened. Add the mushrooms, season with salt and pepper to taste, and cook for 10 minutes.

To serve, place a slice of French bread in each soup bowl. Top each slice with 1 tablespoon grated Gruyère and pour the hot soup over the bread into the bowl.

Summer Squash Soup

(4 servings)

- 4 medium unblemished summer squash, cut into 1-inch slices
- 1 cup water
- 1 cup Chicken Stock or canned chicken broth

Freshly ground black pepper

Put the squash slices, water, and stock or broth in a stainless steel or enamel saucepan. Bring the liquid to a boil, reduce the heat and simmer, covered, until squash is just tender. Remove 8 slices of squash and set aside. Purée the soup in a food mill, blender, or food processor. Return to the pot and reheat slowly; do not boil. Serve the soup with 2 slices of squash in each bowl, garnished with the freshly ground black pepper.

Instant Soups

It isn't necessary to spend hours in the kitchen in order to produce a dazzling soup. A little imagination can turn a can of soup from the grocery store into a tantalizing creation.

First, you must find the product that best compares with homemade soup. Experiment with local and national brands and then stock your pantry shelf with your favorites. Basic "soup starters" include consommé, bouillon, and chicken and beef broth. Some commercial consommés are made with gelatin and can be used as a shortcut in creating aspics and cold jellied soups.

The simplest and fastest instant soup is prepared by refrigerating canned consommé. When ready to serve, pour the soup into chilled glass bowls and garnish with slivers of very finely sliced raw vegetables, such as celery, scallions, or green peppers, and a sprinkling of chopped parsley or fresh dill with a lemon wedge tucked alongside. Or stir in a dash of dry sherry and garnish with a very thin slice of lemon pressed in chopped parsley.

Invest just a little more time in a consommé-based soup and you will have an attention-getter suitable for any gourmet meal. For instance, combine equal quantities of canned turtle and pea soups, and heat. Pour the mixture into ovenproof bowls, top with whipped cream and a layer of Parmesan cheese, and brown lightly under the broiler. The whipped cream and toasted cheese will create a light meringue topping on the creamy pea-green soup.

Two classic Chinese soups, Winter Melon and Corn, based on golden, flavorful chicken broth, are easy to prepare and sure to win honors in the instant-but-exotic class. Winter melon, a pumpkin-size fruit weighing up to five or six pounds, has a light green skin delicately glazed with white "frost." The fruit is sold in one- or two-pound sections in Chinese markets, and will keep carefully wrapped in the refrigerator for up to five days.

The corn soup in this chapter is a variation on the favorite chinese velvet soup, which is made with creamed corn and garnished with cooked ham, chopped chestnuts, and minced chicken, all topped with frothy egg whites. Corn is not indigenous to China and did not arrive there until after World War II; however, the proof is in the tasting that it's been put to good use.

With several well-chosen varieties of canned soups on your shelf, you can indulge in an endless array of flavorful combinations. And be imaginative in your choice of garnishes—toasted almonds, grated orange rind, poached apple slices, diced tomatoes, and any other vegetable cut into pleasing shapes.

Richard Sax's cream of cataloupe soup with coconut and ham

Richard Sax's Cream of Cantaloupe Soup with Coconut & Ham

(6 servings)

2   ripe cantaloupe melons, halved and seeded
3-4 tablespoons dry white wine or dry vermouth
½   cup canned unsweetened coconut cream
3   tablespoons or more fresh lime juice
1   teaspoon salt
½   teaspoon freshly ground white pepper
¼   teaspoon nutmeg
½   cup heavy cream
2   tablespoons orange-flavored liqueur (optional)
Grated zest of 1 lime
2   slices prosciutto, cut in small slivers

Spoon the flesh of the melon into a food mill, blender, or food processor and purée until it is very smooth. Work in batches if necessary.

Put the purée in a serving bowl and stir in the wine or vermouth, coconut cream, lime juice, salt, pepper, nutmeg, and cream. Add the orange liqueur, if desired, and blend the ingredients well. Taste for seasoning and, if necessary, add a bit more of any ingredient. Chill for at least 1 hour to allow the flavors to blend. Garnish the soup with lime zest and slivers of prosciutto.

Elegant Instant Bouillon

(2 servings)

1   10-ounce can beef bouillon
¾   soup can water
¼   cup dry sherry
2   thin slices lemon
Sliced avocado (optional)

In a saucepan heat the bouillon and water. Stir in the sherry. To serve, put a lemon slice in the bottom of a soup cup or mug and pour in the bouillon. Garnish with slices of avocado if desired.

Tomato-Chive Soup

(6 servings)

2 10¾-ounce cans tomato soup
3 cups milk
1 cup heavy cream, *or* Crème Fraîche
1 tablespoon chopped fresh basil
2 teaspoons fresh lemon or lime juice
Pinch celery salt
Freshly ground black pepper
2 tablespoons chopped fresh chives

In an enamel or stainless steel saucepan heat the soup and milk, stirring until they are blended. Remove the pan from the heat and add all other ingredients, except the chives. Chill the soup. Just before serving, sprinkle with chives.

Crab & Tomato Soup

(4 servings)

1 10¾-ounce can tomato soup
2 cups light cream
1 6-ounce can crab meat, flaked

In an enamel or stainless steel saucepan heat the soup and cream, stirring until they are blended. Just before serving, add the crab meat. Serve in warmed bowls with oyster crackers.

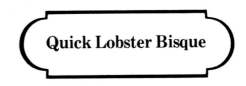

Quick Lobster Bisque

(6 servings)

1 10¾-ounce can cream of mushroom soup
1 10¾-ounce can tomato soup
1 soup can milk
½ soup can light cream
1 6-ounce can lobster meat, flaked
Curry powder to taste
Paprika

Combine all ingredients, except the paprika, in an enamel or stainless steel saucepan. Heat the bisque, stirring, until it is blended. Serve in warmed bowls and sprinkle with paprika.

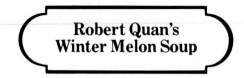

Robert Quan's Winter Melon Soup

(2-4 servings)

- 1 tablespoon oil
- 1 slice peeled gingerroot, about the size of a quarter, ⅛ inch thick, flattened
- 1 scallion, chopped
- 1 10-ounce can chicken broth
- ½ can water
- 1 pound winter melon, peeled, washed, and cut into ½-inch cubes
- 1 4-ounce can button mushrooms
- ½ cup green peas, fresh, or frozen and thawed

Place a wok on its collar over medium heat and add the oil, pouring it in about 2 inches from the top of the wok and rotating the wok until it is well coated. Add the ginger and let it sizzle for about 30 seconds. Add the scallion and toss until just heated. Add the remaining ingredients, bring to a boil, and simmer them for 15 to 20 minutes, or until the peas are cooked and the winter melon is translucent and tender. Remove and discard the ginger before serving.

Curried Apple Soup

(6-8 servings)

- 3 10¾-ounce cans beef consommé
- 2 large apples, unpeeled, cored, and chopped
- 2 medium onions, cut into chunks
- 1½ cups heavy cream
- Salt
- Paprika
- 1 tablespoon or more curry powder

Purée the apples and onions with 1 can consommé in a blender or food processor. In a large saucepan combine the purée and the remaining cans of consommé and simmer the mixture for 15 to 20 minutes. Strain if desired. Add the cream and stir in salt, paprika, and curry powder to taste. Reheat the soup but do not let it boil. Serve warm or very cold.

(Preceding pages) Watercress soup, curried apple soup, Chinese corn soup, Robert Quan's winter melon soup

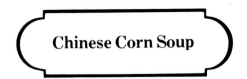

Chinese Corn Soup

(6 servings)

1 16-ounce can cream-style corn
5 cups canned chicken broth
5 tablespoons cornstarch, mixed with 5 tablespoons water
3 egg whites, lightly beaten
2 tablespoons milk
Salt and freshly ground white pepper
Chopped fresh coriander leaves (Chinese parsley) (optional)

In a large saucepan combine the corn and broth and bring to a boil. Stir in the cornstarch paste and heat until the soup is thickened. In a small bowl beat the milk and egg whites together very briefly and skim off the foam from the top of the mixture. Remove the soup from the heat and stir in the egg white mixture. Season the soup with salt and pepper to taste and serve it sprinkled with coriander leaves, if desired.

Quick & Wonderful Watercress Soup

(4 servings)

2 10¾-ounce cans cream of chicken soup
1½ soup cans milk
½ cup sour cream, or Crème Fraîche
1 bunch watercress, tough stems removed (reserve several sprigs for garnish)

Purée all ingredients in a food mill, blender, or food processor. Chill the purée. If the soup is too thick, add more milk. Garnish with reserved sprigs of watercress and serve.

Egg Drop Soup

(4 servings)

2 eggs
2 teaspoons water
1 tablespoon cornstarch, mixed with 2 tablespoons water
6 cups Chicken Stock or canned chicken broth
½ teaspoon sugar
¾ teaspoon salt
1 teaspoon dry sherry
1 tablespoon soy sauce
2 scallions, minced

In a small bowl beat the eggs with the water. In a large saucepan bring the stock or broth to a boil, reduce the heat to moderate, and stir in the sugar, salt, sherry, and soy sauce. Stir in the cornstarch mixture and heat the soup, stirring, until it is thickened. Reduce the heat to low. Pour the beaten eggs in slowly, stirring constantly, until they separate into shreds, and remove the pan from the heat. Sprinkle the soup with the minced scallions and serve.

Tomato-Cucumber Soup

(6-8 servings)

1 10¾-ounce can tomato soup
¾ soup can water
1 medium cucumber peeled, seeded, and cut into 1-inch pieces
Sour cream, *or* Crème Fraîche
Chopped fresh basil or dill

Purée the soup, water, and cucumber in a food mill, blender, or food processor. Chill the purée and serve it with sour cream or crème fraîche sprinkled with basil or dill.

Instant Clam Chowder

(3-4 servings)

1   15½-oz can of whole tomatoes in tomato puree
1   6¾-oz can of minced clams, including their liquor
1   cup water
1   small carrot, sliced
1   stalk celery, chopped
1   small onion, chopped
1   clove garlic, minced
¼   teaspoon dried oregano
½   teaspoon chopped fresh basil or ¼ teaspoon dried
2   teaspoons chopped fresh parsley or ¾ teaspoon dried
    Freshly ground black pepper

Combine all the ingredients in a stainless steel or enamel saucepan and bring to a boil. Reduce the heat and simmer, covered, for about 10 minutes, or until the vegetables are tender. Serve with oyster crackers.

Pizza Soup

(2 servings)

1   15½-oz can whole tomatoes in tomato puree
1   cup water
¼   teaspoon dried oregano
½   teaspoon chopped fresh basil or ¼ teaspoon dried
¼   teaspoon garlic powder
1   tablespoon finely minced onion or 1 teaspoon dried
4   teaspoons coarsely grated mozzarella cheese
2   tablespoons grated Parmesan cheese

Combine the tomatoes and puree, water, oregano, basil, garlic and onion in a stainless steel or enamel saucepan and bring to a boil. Simmer, covered, for 10 minutes. Place the soup into bowls, top with the cheeses, and serve.

Salads

What would *SMALL FEASTS* be without Salads? From the simple to the elaborate, salads are accompaniments, main dishes, refreshing interludes, even desserts.

The basics are Green Salads and Dressings; a green salad with a well-chosen dressing is the perfect complement for soups and sandwiches. Dressings are also used to combine ingredients in more substantial salads. In this chapter you will find dressings to suit all manner of ingredients for all manner of salads—dressings for greens, for vegetables, for fruit, for seafood, for meats and chicken in appealing and satisfying combinations.

Stuffed Vegetables and Fruits are wonderful salads to serve for parties. Ingredients can be prepared the night before and assembled right before the guests arrive. Here are recipes, for example, to help you elevate tomatoes from the realm of standard fare with fillings of Smoked Salmon or Curried Chicken, or by combining Cherry Tomatoes with Avocado.

Many of the Vegetable Salads are perfect for picnics; choose from several versions of potato salads and slaws, for example. Others, such as Tiered Vegetable Salad, for one, are easy and elegant accompaniments to substantial entrées—appealing to the eye as well as pleasing to the palate.

Seafood Salads and Meat and Poultry Salads can be satisfying and substantial, or light and refreshing—as basic as Macaroni & Meat Salad, as sophisticated as Duck & Orange Salad, as creative as Chicken Salad Español. Many meat and poultry salads can be prepared with leftovers, or planned for in advance when other meat and poultry dishes are cooked.

Molded Salads are a challenge and an opportunity. Easy when you know the tricks (this chapter tells all), these salads are wonderful light entrées for lunch, impressive additions to any buffet.

Perfectly suited to the requirements of today's trend toward light cuisine, Fruit Salads are a real pleasure. Have your lunch and have dessert, all in the same satisfying Fruit Salad Platter or Banana Split Salad.

Enjoy a simple salad or an elegant one, as a main dish or an accompaniment. Or enjoy a range of salads in a spectacular Salad Bar Buffet.

ONE
Dressings & Greens

Salad Dressings

No matter how magnificent your salad may be on its own, a complementary dressing will add immeasurably to its appeal. The very best of green salads need light, subtle dressings to enhance their flavors. More substantial salads need dressings too, to blend their ingredients and to add special accents.

There are endless salad dressing possibilities, but most are variations on two basic types, vinaigrette and mayonnaise. Vinaigrette, sometimes called French dressing, combines oil with vinegar and can be varied almost infinitely with the selection of herbs and spices for specific flavors. Mayonnaise combines oil with an emulsion of egg yolks, and we propose a speedy blender-made version. Mayonnaise also combines well with additional ingredients for many splendid variations. A third type of salad dressing is based on dairy products, such as yogurt, cheese, and sour cream. Many of this type are fairly low in calories and high in protein—a special plus.

You can vary dressings to suit individual tastes as well as specific salads. Using different oils will produce dressings that differ in taste and texture from basic recipes. "Salad oil" (blended vegetable oil) is only one of an increasing array of alternatives. Others include rich virgin olive oil (from the first pressing); lighter oils, such as corn, peanut, or safflower; more delicately flavored oils—walnut, hazelnut, even apricot. Vinegars abound as well: wine, white or red; cider; tarragon; shallot- or garlic-flavored; and mild rice vinegar. Some, however, such as red-wine vinegar, are high in acid and may need tempering to suit your taste: extra oil, perhaps a pinch of white sugar; or lemon juice may be used instead of vinegar.

A vinaigrette should not be made too far in advance. Mayonnaise is best when fresh, too. If premixing is unavoidable, store the dressing, covered, in the refrigerator. Serve it at room temperature on well-dried, slightly chilled greens. Remember, too, that a salad dressed too early or too heavily soon becomes limp. One caution about mayonnaise and its variations should be observed without fail. It will harbor increasing numbers of bacteria—the common cause of food poisoning—as it becomes warm. If you include dishes prepared with mayonnaise in a picnic or lawn party menu, be sure they are refrigerated or stored in ice-filled hampers until ready to serve.

Vinaigrette

(½ cup)

- 2 tablespoons red- or white-wine vinegar
- 6-8 tablespoons olive oil
- ½ teaspoon salt
- ¾ teaspoon Dijon mustard
- 2 teaspoons finely chopped shallots (optional)
  Freshly ground black pepper

Blend all the ingredients, except the pepper, in a blender or food processor, or in a jar with a tight-fitting lid, until the mixture is well combined. Transfer the dressing to a container and add pepper to taste.

NOTE: For a lighter dressing, combine 3 to 4 tablespoons olive oil and 3 to 4 tablespoons salad oil.

WITH AVOCADO: Beat ½ mashed avocado (approximately ½ cup) into 1 cup Vinaigrette. Serve the dressing immediately on sliced tomatoes or citrus fruit salad.

WITH CAPERS: Add ⅓ cup finely chopped capers to 1 cup Vinaigrette. Drizzle over sliced tomatoes, fish, or poultry salad.

WITH CHIVES: Add 1 tablespoon each of chopped fresh chives and finely chopped shallots or onion to 1 cup Vinaigrette.

WITH CUCUMBER: Add 3 tablespoons grated cucumber and 1 tablespoon chopped fresh chives to 1 cup Vinaigrette.

WITH CURRY: Add ¼ teaspoon curry powder and 1 tablespoon finely chopped scallions or shallots to 1 cup Vinaigrette.

WITH GARLIC: In a blender or food processor blend 1 cup Vinaigrette with 1 clove garlic for 10 seconds. Or let the garlic marinate in the dressing in the refrigerator overnight. Remove the garlic before serving.

WITH HERBS: Add 3 sprigs parsley, finely chopped, 1 teaspoon dried tarragon, and 1 teaspoon fresh basil or ½ teaspoon dried to 1 cup Vinaigrette.

WITH SESAME SEEDS: Preheat the oven to 350°. On a baking sheet toast ¼ cup sesame seeds for 15 minutes. Or sauté them in 1 tablespoon olive oil until they are lightly browned. Add the sesame seeds and 1 small garlic clove, finely chopped, to 1 cup Vinaigrette.

TARRAGON VINAIGRETTE: Substitute tarragon vinegar for the red- or white-wine vinegar in the master recipe.

VINAIGRETTE CHIFFONADE: Add 1 tablespoon each of chopped pickled beets, drained; chopped green olives, drained; chopped fresh chives; chopped parsley; and 2 hard-boiled eggs, coarsely chopped, to 1 cup Vinaigrette.

Michel Guérard's Sauce Vinaigrette Minceur I

(½ cup, or 4 servings)

- 1 tablespoon olive oil
- 5 tablespoons Chicken Stock
- 1 tablespoon red-wine vinegar
- 1 tablespoon fresh lemon juice
- Salt and pepper

In a small bowl combine the ingredients and mix well with a fork.

NOTE: For Vinaigrettes, you should use homemade stock, which has the gelatin content lacking in canned or bouillon cube broths.

Michel Guérard's Sauce Vinaigrette Minceur II

(½ cup, or 4 servings)

- 1 tablespoon olive oil
- 5 tablespoons Chicken Stock
- 1 clove garlic
- ½ teaspoon minced fresh chervil or parsley
- 2 leaves fresh basil, minced
- 1 tablespoon sherry vinegar
- 1 tablespoon fresh lemon juice
- Salt and pepper

In a small bowl combine the olive oil, stock, garlic, and herbs and let them marinate for 2 hours. Add the vinegar, lemon juice, and salt and pepper and mix well with a fork.

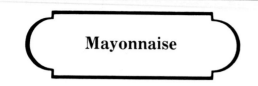

Mayonnaise

(1¼ cups)

- 1 egg
- 1½ tablespoons fresh lemon juice, *or* white-wine vinegar, *or* a combination of both
- 1 teaspoon Dijon mustard
- ¼ teaspoon freshly ground white pepper
- 1 cup olive oil or salad oil or a combination of both

Blend the egg, lemon juice or vinegar, mustard, salt, and pepper together in a blender or food processor for 30 seconds. With the motor still running add the oil in a slow steady stream and blend until the oil in incorporated and the mixture is thickened. If the mayonnaise seems too thick, thin it with a little water or heavy cream. Adjust the seasonings to taste and serve the dressing immediately or place in a tightly covered jar and store it in the refrigerator for up to 7 days. If the mayonnaise separates, bring to room temperature and stir gently.

CURRY MAYONNAISE: Combine 1 cup Mayonnaise with 1½ teaspoons curry powder and 1 small clove garlic, mashed, and stir the mixture until it is well blended. Serve with egg, potato, artichoke, tomato, poultry, or seafood salad.

DILL MAYONNAISE: Fold ⅓ cup sour cream into 2 cups Mayonnaise. Add ⅓ cup snipped fresh dill, 2 teaspoons Dijon mustard, and 1 teaspoon anchovy paste. If desired, add 1 clove garlic, finely chopped, and stir until well blended. Use on bean, cucumber, or egg salad.

HERB MAYONNAISE: Combine 1 cup Mayonnaise with 1 tablespoon of one or a combination of all of the following finely chopped fresh herbs: parsley, basil, tarragon, chives. One tablespoon dried oregano can also be added. Stir until well combined. Serve with macaroni, vegetable, meat, seafood, or egg salad.

Russian Dressing

(1½ cups)

- ½ cup Mayonnaise
- ½ cup sour cream
- 3 tablespoons chili sauce
- 3 tablespoons fresh lime juice
- 2 tablespoons finely chopped fresh chives
- ¼ teaspoon salt

In a bowl combine all the ingredients and stir until well blended. Refrigerate the dressing before serving. Serve with seafood salads.

Thousand Island Dressing

(3 cups)

- 1 cup Mayonnaise
- ½ cup chili sauce
- 3 hard-boiled eggs, finely chopped
- ¼ cup green pickle relish, *or* 2 tablespoons finely chopped pimiento-stuffed green olives
- ⅓ cup finely chopped green pepper
- ⅓ cup finely chopped celery
- 1 small onion or 2 whole scallions, finely chopped
- 2 teaspoons finely chopped parsley

In a bowl combine well all the ingredients. Chill the dressing until ready to serve.

Pontchartrain Dressing

(4 cups)

- 1 teaspoon sugar
- ¾ teaspoon dry mustard
- ¼ teaspoon cayenne
- 1 cup cider vinegar
- 3 cups salad oil
- 1 teaspoon salt
- ½ teaspoon freshly ground black pepper
- ½ clove garlic, minced

Combine all the ingredients, except the garlic, in a jar with a tight-fitting lid. Shake well and add the garlic. Serve on tossed green salads.

Green Goddess Dressing

(2 cups)

- 6 anchovy fillets
- 1 clove garlic
- 1 small onion or 2 scallions, coarsely chopped
- 1 cup Mayonnaise
- ⅔ cup heavy cream
- ¼ cup white-wine vinegar or tarragon vinegar
- 2 tablespoons fresh lemon juice
- ½ cup chopped parsley
- ¼ teaspoon freshly ground black pepper
- Salt

Blend all the ingredients, except the salt, in a blender or food processor until smooth. Pour the dressing into a bowl and chill it, covered, for at least 5 hours. Add salt to taste and serve with green salad or with chicken, crab-meat, or shrimp salads.

Cream Cheese Dressing

(¾ cup)

- 3 ounces cream cheese, softened
- 2 teaspoons honey
- 2 teaspoons fresh lemon juice
- 3 tablespoons fresh orange juice
- ¼ teaspoon salt

In a bowl combine the cheese, honey, and salt. Stir in the lemon juice and orange juice, and beat until smooth. Serve with fruit salad.

Sour Cream & Honey Dressing

(1 cup)

- 1 cup sour cream
- 2 tablespoons honey
- 1½ teaspoons fresh lemon juice
- Salt

In a bowl combine all the ingredients, except the salt, and mix until blended. Add salt to taste and chill. Serve with fruit salads.

WITH ORANGE RIND: Add ¼ teaspoon grated orange rind.

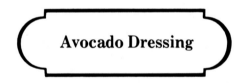

Avocado Dressing

(2 cups)

- 1 cup mashed avocado
- 1 cup sour cream
- 2 tablespoons sugar
- 2 tablespoons fresh lime juice
- Freshly ground white pepper

Blend all the ingredients, except the pepper, in a blender or food processor until well combined and add pepper to taste. Serve with fruit salads.

NOTE: Make this dressing just before you are ready to serve the salad. If prepared in advance, the avocado will discolor.

Cinnamon Yogurt Dressing

(1 cup)

- 1 cup plain yogurt
- 1½ tablespoons confectioners' sugar
- ¼ teaspoon cinnamon
- 1 tablespoon finely chopped fresh mint

Place the yogurt in a bowl and beat in the sugar and cinnamon until well blended. Fold in the mint and chill. Serve with fruit salads.

Fruit salad with sour cream and honey dressing

Chutney Dressing

(2 cups)

1 cup salad oil
⅓ cup cider vinegar
¼ teaspoon paprika
¾ cup sugar
1 clove garlic, minced
2 tablespoons ketchup
1 tablespoon fresh lemon juice
1½ teaspoons Worcestershire sauce
¼ cup chutney, chopped
1 teaspoon curry powder
1½ teaspoons salt
Freshly ground black pepper

In a bowl combine all ingredients and mix until thoroughly blended. Serve with fruit salads.

Roquefort Dressing I

(2½ cups)

1 cup Mayonnaise
1 cup sour cream
1 teaspoon garlic salt
1 teaspoon celery salt
2 tablespoons fresh lemon juice, *or* white-wine vinegar
4 ounces Roquefort, crumbled

In a bowl combine all the ingredients and refrigerate until ready to serve.

Roquefort Dressing II

(1½ cups)

⅔ cup salad oil or olive oil
3 tablespoons fresh lemon juice
1 clove garlic
1 tablespoon Worcestershire sauce
4 ounces Roquefort, crumbled

Blend all the ingredients in a blender or food processor for 1 minute. Serve on green salads.

Mustard Yogurt Dressing

(1¼ cups)

1 cup plain yogurt
1 tablespoon Dijon mustard
2 tablespoons salad oil
1 tablespoon tarragon vinegar
1 tablespoon chopped parsley

In a bowl mix all the ingredients until blended. Chill. Serve with spinach, watercress, or beet salad.

Lemon Yogurt Dressing

(1¼ cups)

½ cup plain yogurt
Scant ¼ cup fresh lemon juice
½ cup creamed cottage cheese
1 teaspoon salt
½ teaspoon paprika
½ green pepper, finely chopped
Freshly ground white pepper

Blend thoroughly all the ingredients, except the green pepper and white pepper, in a blender or food processor. Transfer to a bowl, stir in the green pepper, add white pepper to taste, and chill. Serve with seafood salads.

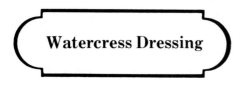

Watercress Dressing

(Approximately 1¾ cups)

½ cup firmly packed watercress leaves
1 tablespoon sugar
2-3 leeks (white parts only), cut into pieces
¼ cup cider vinegar
1 cup salad oil
Salt and freshly ground black pepper

Purée the watercress, sugar, leeks, and vinegar in a blender or food processor until liquefied. With the motor running add the oil in a stream, slowly, and blend until incorporated. Add salt and pepper to taste and serve with vegetable salads.

Sour Cream Dressing

(1½ cups)

½ cup Mayonnaise
1 cup sour cream
½ cup chopped parsley
2 tablespoons cider vinegar or white-wine vinegar
1 small onion, chopped
Salt and freshly ground white pepper
Worcestershire sauce

Blend all the ingredients in a blender or food processor until well combined. Serve with vegetable or potato salad.

Green Salads

The seemingly small selection of salads in this section is actually an infinite variety, for mixed green salads are remarkably versatile. Though you will undoubtedly enjoy preparing and sampling Caesar Salad, Greek Salad, or Wilted Lettuce Salad, you may find the catalogue of greens in the basic Green Salad recipe—greens you have seen at the produce stand or in the supermarket but may not have tried—even more interesting. You can combine these greens to create salads that vary widely in taste and texture, some subtle, some strong, to accompany almost any soup or sandwich. Perk up a salad with arrugula or dandelion greens to complement a subtle soup or simple sandwich. Rely on Bibb or Boston lettuce with a light and creamy dressing to accompany a highly seasoned heartier dish.

Whatever you choose, select your greens with care. Inspect each head of lettuce. Choose only those that are firm and bright in color. Avoid any greens that are limp and discolored. Only the freshest of greens can be counted on to lend the crisp texture that is so essential to a green salad. Try not to shop too far in advance of the preparation of your salad. If greens are not to be used immediately, store them in the vegetable compartment of your refrigerator, making sure that the bottom of the drawer is dry. Do not wash them until you begin preparing the salad; they will stay crisp in the meantime. Watercress, parsley, scallions, and other cut herbs keep best chilled, with the stems in water. After washing, refrigerate them standing in partially filled glasses.

To prepare greens for your salad, trim them, discard wilted outer leaves, then rinse under cold running water. Some greens, particularly spinach, chicory and dandelion, should be rinsed in a sinkful of cold water to remove grit.

Washed greens should be thoroughly dried, since excess moisture may spoil the texture of your dressing. You can dry them with paper or kitchen towels, or use a salad spinner—a basket within a basket that spins to dry greens. Assemble your salad and dress it lightly just before serving. Toss in some croutons. Or add mimosa—sieved hard-boiled egg yolks—as a subtle but sensational crowning touch.

Basic Green Salad

(4 servings)

4   cups assorted salad greens, well chilled

⅓-½   cup dressing

The actual preparation of a green salad is simplicity itself. Assemble the greens in a bowl, breaking them into pieces or, if they are small, leaving them whole.

Produce is seasonal, but cross-country trucking and refrigerated trains provide summer-fresh greens anytime, anywhere. You will find healthful and interesting choices all year round at your greengrocer and specialty food stores. And when local produce is in season, so many greens will be available at roadside stands or markets in your area it will be hard for you to choose.

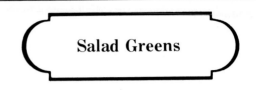

Salad Greens

These are some of the greens that will make wonderful salads:

ARRUGULA: A flat-leafed green, somewhat bitter in taste. Considered a specialty in some parts of the country, it is found most frequently in Italian markets.

BELGIAN ENDIVE: A pale green, almost white, stalk of long, tightly packed leaves. Endive, which is also called witloof chicory, is part of the chicory family, crisp and crunchy, and slightly bitter in flavor. It is much more expensive than most kinds of lettuce. Endive, dressed with walnut oil and vinegar, makes a very elegant salad.

BIBB LETTUCE: A small, tightly packed head, pale in color and sweet in flavor.

BOSTON LETTUCE: A not-so-tightly packed pale green head, delicate in taste.

CHICORY OR CURLY ENDIVE: A larger head of lettuce, deeper in color than either Bibb or Boston. Chicory is bitter in taste, and easily identifiable by its curly leaves. It is best when used in combination with other greens.

DANDELION GREENS: Wild, or commercially grown, these have a bitter taste, and are usually dark in color. An interesting accent for a mixed salad.

ESCAROLE: This green looks somewhat like chicory, and is similarly strong in flavor.

ICEBERG LETTUCE: Although it may seem fashionable to reject this ubiquitous, perhaps overfamiliar lettuce, it is reliable, has a satisfying texture, and is readily available in any season. It also keeps well—and has recently been featured in a chic gourmet shop in Paris, as a new American delicacy!

LEAF LETTUCE: The heads are leafy, large, and a glowing lime-green color. *Red*-leaf lettuce has amber-colored borders on its leaves. Mild, even sweet in flavor, leaf lettuce is not easy to find, but well worth the extra time it takes to turn it up. And worth the extra pennies you will have to pay for it, even in season.

ROMAINE LETTUCE: This popular lettuce, staple for the Caesar Salad, has long broad leaves that range from dark green to pale yellow from the outside to the center of the head. The inner leaves are small and fragile, and particularly delicate in flavor.

SPINACH: The leaves are dark green and curly, and grow on a long stem. Spinach leaves can range from large to small in size. The stems should be removed when preparing salads with this green. The distinct flavor of spinach is complemented by pungent salad dressings.

WATERCRESS: Generally thought of as a garnish, or as the dainty filling in fragile bread-and-butter tea sandwiches, watercress has a lively flavor and mixes well with other greens. Remember to trim off the tough stems, though, and use only the leafy sections.

(Overleaf) Chicory, endive, watercress, bibb lettuce, spinach, romaine, Boston lettuce, escarole, iceberg lettuce, red-leaf lettuce

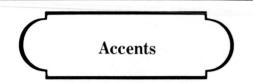

Accents

The basic salad greens can be combined any way you wish and enhanced by countless finishing touches. Among the following you are sure to find many that will become personal favorites.

GARLIC: Some feel a little goes a long way. Others like the taste of it. For a delicate hint of garlic, rub the inside of a wooden salad bowl with a cut garlic clove before you assemble your greens in it. For a little garlic flavor, use a garlic press and add the pressed pulp to your dressing. For a real taste of garlic, mince it fine and add it to your greens.

HERBS: A sprinkling of herbs can make a simple salad really special. If you can get fresh herbs—or grow your own on a windowsill—chopped parsley, snipped chives or dill, minced basil, tarragon, or mint leaves will make a delicious addition to almost any salad. If only dried herbs are on hand, try a combination of oregano and tarragon, or chervil and sage. Experiment. But remember that dried herbs are much stronger in flavor than fresh ones, so use them judiciously or they will overpower your greens.

ONIONS: Finely chopped red or yellow onions are a perfect accent for a green salad.

Thin slices, or rings, of red or yellow onion are another attractive topping for a bed of greens. In addition, you might include slender slices of scallion along with some of their deep green tops. Finely minced shallots will contribute a subtle, garlicky flavor.

TOMATOES: Consider whole cherry tomatoes, stemmed, or cut a large tomato into wedges. Some chefs insist that for a truly elegant salad the tomatoes must be peeled. Peel tomatoes by plunging them into boiling water for about 10 seconds, which loosens the skins. Put them in cold water to cool, then remove the skins with a sharp paring knife. Cut tomatoes should be added to a salad at the last minute; their juices tend to wilt the greens.

COLORFUL ACCENTS: Try adding other vegetables in small amounts to enhance your green salad with colors and textures. Thin slices of carrot might be the perfect contrast in a bowl of greens. Shredded red cabbage, thin slices of radish, slices of cucumber, slices or rings of green or red pepper will also add color and crunch.

Greek Salad

Wilted Lettuce Salad

(4-6 servings)

6-8	cups salad greens
2	tomatoes, seeded and cut into wedges
1	green pepper, sliced crosswise into thin rings
1	small red onion, thinly sliced
8	Greek olives or other black olives
6	tablespoons olive oil
2	tablespoons fresh lemon juice, *or* red-wine vinegar
1	teaspoon dried oregano

Salt and freshly ground black pepper
¼-½ cup crumbled feta cheese

Crisp the lettuce, wrapped in damp paper towels or a kitchen towel, in the refrigerator. Break the leaves into bite-size pieces and put them in a chilled salad bowl. Add the tomatoes, pepper, onion, and olives.

In a small bowl combine the oil, lemon juice or vinegar, oregano, and salt and pepper to taste. Beat until well blended. Pour the dressing over the salad and toss gently. Sprinkle with the cheese before serving.

MINT VARIATION: For a distinct and refreshing taste substitute 2 tablespoons fresh mint for the oregano.

(6 servings)

4	slices bacon
2	heads lettuce (romaine, Boston, escarole), *or* spinach
3	tablespoons finely chopped scallion, including some of the green tops
3	hard-boiled eggs, chopped
4	tablespoons vinegar, *or* fresh lemon juice
1	teaspoon sugar
½	teaspoon Dijon mustard

Salt and freshly ground black pepper

In a skillet cook the bacon until crisp and reserve the fat. Drain the bacon on paper towels and crumble it.

Crisp the lettuce or spinach, wrapped in paper towels or a kitchen towel, in the refrigerator. Break the leaves into pieces and put them in a chilled salad bowl with the scallion, eggs, and bacon. To the reserved fat in the skillet add the vinegar, sugar, mustard, and salt and pepper to taste and heat until the sugar dissolves. Pour the dressing over the salad, toss, and serve immediately.

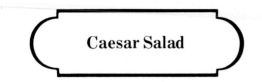

Caesar Salad

(4 servings)

    2-3 large heads romaine lettuce
    ¾   cup olive oil
    Salt and freshly ground black pepper
    2   eggs, boiled 1 minute
    3   tablespoons fresh lemon juice
    6   drops Worcestershire sauce
    6   tablespoons freshly grated
         Parmesan
    8   anchovy fillets (optional)

Cube enough day-old French bread to make 2 cups. In a skillet heat ½ cup olive oil or vegetable oil and when it is hot add 1 large clove garlic, crushed, and sauté until it is lightly browned. Remove the garlic, add the bread cubes, and sauté until they are golden. Transfer the croutons to paper towels to drain.

Separate the leaves of the lettuce, reserving the outer leaves for another use. Wash the tender pale green inner leaves, pat them dry, and wrap them in damp paper towels or a kitchen towel and place in the refrigerator to crisp. Break the lettuce into bite-size pieces, put it in a chilled salad bowl, and sprinkle over it the olive oil and salt and pepper to taste. Toss the salad gently. Break the eggs into the bowl and add the lemon juice, Worcestershire sauce, cheese, and the anchovies, if desired. Toss again and add the croutons. Serve immediately.

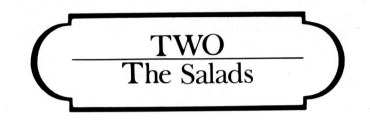

TWO
The Salads

Stuffed Fruits & Vegetables

For company dishes that are fun, impressive, and easier to make than you might think, try fruits or vegetables stuffed with salads. Think of the tomato, the avocado, the celery stalk, artichoke bottom, grapefruit, lemon, melon, or watermelon rind in a new way: as a container.

Consider melon boats filled with curried tuna, lemons stuffed with herring salad, celery stuffed with cheese, avocados filled with seafood salad, tomatoes brimming with smoked salmon or curried chicken. One tomato salad is a real surprise—cherry tomatoes stuffed with avocado. The salads in this section vary in texture and flavor. Some are hearty and others are light. Avocados with seafood salad is a lovely luncheon dish; curried chicken and pasta in tomatoes is substantial enough for a hearty meal.

Some vegetable containers are more difficult to prepare properly than others. If you are using tomatoes, be sure they are firm. Only ripe avocados will do, and beware of trying to prepare them in advance; they will discolor almost immediately. Lemon juice rubbed on all cut avocado surfaces will retard darkening, but only temporarily. Any salad made with mayonnaise should, of course, be refrigerated until it is to be served.

To make these dishes even more attractive, "sawtooth" hollowed-out fruits and vegetables before stuffing. It is easily accomplished. Simply trim the edges of citrus fruit rinds, melon rinds, even tomatoes or peppers, into little triangular sawteeth all around.

In addition to the fruits and vegetables in this section, you will find two new recipes for a familiar dish: stuffed eggs. Hearty versions of an old buffet standby, Curried Stuffed Eggs or Eggs Stuffed with Ham make an appealing first course, or perhaps a dish for a simple brunch or light luncheon.

These recipes, some basic, some sophisticated, may spark ideas for your own culinary creations. Experiment with salad combinations and containers for a unique buffet for a small gathering. You can prepare the fillings and containers in advance and assemble the salads at the last minute.

Avocados with seafood salad

Avocados with Seafood Salad

(4 servings)

- 1 cup chilled, cooked lobster, crab meat, or shrimp, cut into bite-size pieces
- 2 hard-boiled eggs, coarsely chopped
- ½ cup chopped celery
- Salt and freshly ground black pepper
- 1½ cups Russian Dressing or Mayonnaise
- 2 large ripe avocados
- Fresh lemon juice
- Tomato slices (optional)

In a mixing bowl combine the shell fish, eggs, celery, and salt and pepper to taste with ½ cup of the dressing or mayonnaise. Toss gently and chill, covered.

Just before serving, halve the avocados lengthwise, remove the pits, and rub the cut sides with the lemon juice. Place each avocado half on a plate, fill it with some of the shellfish mixture, and garnish with tomato slices, if desired. Serve with the remaining dressing or mayonnaise.

NOTE: Ripe avocado should be used at once as it does not keep well. If ripe ones are unavailable, you can purchase a firm avocado but allow 1 to 3 days for it to ripen at room temperature.

GRAPEFRUIT VARIATION: Cut the sections of 1 large grapefruit into pieces to measure 1 cup. In a bowl combine them with ½ cup Russian Dressing, toss gently, and chill. Fill the avocados and serve them as in the master recipe.

Tomatoes Stuffed with Curried Chicken & Pasta

(4 servings)

- 4 firm ripe tomatoes
- 1 cup cold diced chicken
- 2 cups cold cooked macaroni
- ¾ cup Mayonnaise
- ¼ cup plain yogurt
- 1½ teaspoons curry powder
- Salt and white pepper
- Chopped parsley
- Raw mushrooms, sliced

Cut off the tops of the tomatoes and with a small spoon scoop out the insides. Invert to drain and chill.

In a bowl combine the chicken, macaroni, mayonnaise, yogurt, and curry powder and add salt and pepper to taste. On a platter garnished with mushroom slices arrange the tomatoes, fill them, and sprinkle with chopped parsley. Serve at once.

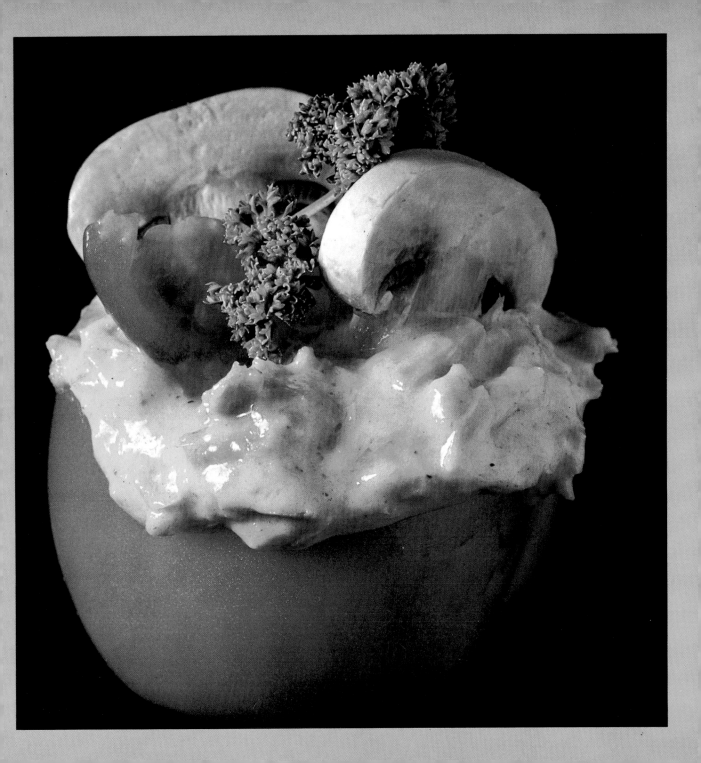

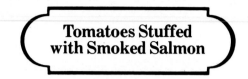

Tomatoes Stuffed with Smoked Salmon

(4 servings)

- 4 firm ripe tomatoes
- 1 large cucumber, peeled, halved lengthwise, and seeded
- ½ teaspoon salt
- ¼ pound thinly sliced smoked salmon, cut into ½-inch squares
- ½ cup sour cream
- ½ tablespoon capers, drained
- 2 scallions, including some of the green tops, finely chopped
- ½ teaspoon finely chopped fresh dill
- 1½ tablespoons tarragon vinegar

Freshly ground black pepper

Cut off the tops of the tomatoes and with a small spoon scoop out the insides. Invert to drain and chill.

Cut the cucumber into ½-inch slices, sprinkle the slices with the salt, and let them stand for 30 minutes. Rinse under cold running water, drain, and dry thoroughly.

In a bowl mix the salmon with the cucumber and add the remaining ingredients. Adjust the seasonings as desired. Chill, covered, for several hours. Before serving, fill each tomato with some of the salmon mixture and garnish each with additional dill.

Cherry Tomatoes Stuffed with Avocado

(4-6 servings)

- 30 cherry tomatoes
- ½ teaspoon salt
- ½ teaspoon sugar
- 2 medium avocados
- 2 tablespoons heavy cream
- 2 tablespoons finely chopped parsley
- 4 teaspoons fresh lime juice
- 2 teaspoons fresh lemon juice
- 2 teaspoons finely chopped fresh chives

Hot pepper sauce

Salad greens

Watercress leaves

Cut a thin slice from the stem end of each cherry tomato and scoop out the flesh and seeds with a melon ball cutter. Discard the tops of the tomatoes. Sprinkle the insides with salt and sugar, invert the tomatoes, and let them drain for 40 minutes.

Cut each avocado in half lengthwise, scoop out the pulp with a silver spoon, and mash it in a bowl. Add the remaining ingredients, except the greens, and mix well. Divide the filling among the tomatoes. Serve on a platter of salad greens garnished with the watercress.

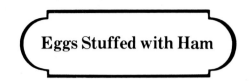

Eggs Stuffed with Ham

(4 servings)

- 4 hard-boiled eggs
- 1 ounce boiled ham, minced
- 1 tablespoon Dijon mustard
- 2 tablespoons butter, softened
- ¼ teaspoon Worcestershire sauce
- 2 teaspoons Mayonnaise
- 1 tablespoon chopped fresh chives
- Salt and freshly ground black pepper
- Salad greens
- Green pimiento-stuffed olives, sliced

Halve the eggs lengthwise and remove the yolks. In a bowl combine the yolks with the ham, mustard, and butter and blend thoroughly. Stir in the Worcestershire sauce, mayonnaise, chives, and salt and pepper to taste. Fill each egg white half with some of the mixture and garnish it with olive slices. Serve the halves as a first course on a platter lined with salad greens.

CHEESE VARIATION: Substitute ¼ cup crumbled blue cheese and ½ cup cream cheese, softened, for the ham in the master recipe. Fill the egg whites with mixture and serve on a plate garnished with quartered cherry tomatoes.

Curried Stuffed Eggs

(4 servings)

- 1 tablespoon finely chopped onion
- 3 tablespoons butter, softened
- 1 teaspoon curry powder
- ¼ cup heavy cream
- 4 hard-boiled eggs
- Salt and freshly ground black pepper
- Bits of chutney

In a small skillet or saucepan sauté the onion in 1 tablespoon of the butter over moderate heat until tender but not browned. Add the curry powder, cook for 10 seconds, and stir in the cream. Bring just to a boil, remove from the heat, and let cool.

Halve the eggs lengthwise and remove the yolks. In a bowl combine the yolks with the curry mixture and the remaining butter, add salt and pepper to taste, and blend thoroughly. Divide the mixture among the whites. Garnish the halves with a dollop of chutney and serve.

Artichoke Bottoms with Mushroom Mayonnaise

(4 servings)

1   cup Mayonnaise
1   cup sour cream
1   tablespoon dry sherry
2   tablespoons fresh lemon juice
½   teaspoon hot pepper sauce
4   tablespoons tomato paste
Salt and freshly ground white pepper
1   pound mushrooms, sliced and
     sprinkled with a little lemon juice to
     prevent discoloration
8   large canned artichoke bottoms,
     drained
Shredded lettuce
Chopped parsley

In a glass bowl combine all the ingredients except the artichoke bottoms and mushrooms, and mix well. Add the mushroom slices and toss gently. Let the mixture marinate, covered, for several hours in the refrigerator.

On a platter lined with the lettuce fill each artichoke bottom with some of the mixture and garnish with the parsley.

Celery Cheese Salad

(6 servings)

1   bunch celery
8   ounces cream cheese, softened
2-3 pimientos, drained and chopped
Salt and freshly ground black pepper
Salad greens
1½   cups Thousand Island Dressing
       (optional)

Separate the celery stalks and rinse and dry each thoroughly. Trim the root ends and leaves and cut the stalks into equal lengths.

In a bowl combine the cream cheese, pimientos, and salt and pepper to taste and blend thoroughly. Fill each stalk with some of the cheese filling. Put the stalks on a plate, and cover with plastic wrap. Chill the celery for several hours. Before serving, cut the celery into ½-inch slices. Arrange the celery on a platter lined with salad greens and serve it with dressing, if desired.

NOTE: Reserve the root ends and leaves to use in soups or stews.

Artichoke bottom with mushroom mayonnaise

Lemons Stuffed
with Herring Salad

(6 servings)

6	large lemons
1	8-ounce jar pickled herring in wine sauce
3	large potatoes, boiled and diced (about 3 cups diced)
3	medium tart green apples, peeled, cored, and chopped (about 2 cups chopped)
1	cup diced cooked beets
3	dill pickles, chopped
1	medium onion, finely chopped
2	tablespoons finely chopped parsley
2	hard-boiled eggs, chopped

½-¾ cup Vinaigrette
Salad greens
Additional beet slices

Make a ½-inch cap for each lemon by cutting off the stem end. Reserve the caps. Cut a thin slice off the other end of each lemon, so that each stands upright. Hollow out the lemons with a small spoon and discard the pulp.

In a glass bowl combine the remaining ingredients, except the salad greens and sliced beets, and toss gently. Fill each lemon with some of the mixture and top with a lemon cap. Serve the stuffed lemons on a platter lined with salad greens and surround them with the sliced beets.

SARDINE SALAD VARIATION: Mash 2 4-ounce cans boneless sardines, drained, with 2 hard-boiled eggs and add ½ to ¾ cup Mayonnaise. Mix well and add salt and fresh lemon juice to taste. Fill each lemon shell with some of the sardine mixture and serve the lemons on a bed of salad greens.

Curried Tuna Salad
in Melon Boats

(4 servings)

2	7-ounce cans water-packed tuna, drained and flaked
1¼	cup coarsely chopped walnuts
1	cup finely chopped celery
¼	cup finely chopped onion
½	cup Mayonnaise
1-2	teaspoons fresh lemon or lime juice
½	teaspoon curry powder

Salt
2 large cantaloupes, halved
Sprigs parsley

About 1 hour before serving, in a bowl combine the tuna, walnuts, celery, onion, and mayonnaise, toss gently, and add the lemon or lime juice, curry powder, and salt to taste. Toss again, cover, and chill. Just before serving, divide the tuna filling among the melon halves and garnish the halves with parsley sprigs.

Pears Stuffed with Dates

(6 servings)

- 4 cups cold water
- 1 tablespoon fresh lemon juice
- 6 firm unblemished pears
- 1 cup sugar
- 3 2-inch strips orange peel
- 3 ounces cream cheese, softened
- 1 tablespoon honey
- ¼ teaspoon salt
- 2 teaspoons fresh lemon juice
- 1 teaspoon grated orange rind
- ¾ cup pitted and sliced fresh dates
- Salad greens
- 2 teaspoons toasted slivered almonds

In a nonmetallic bowl combine the water and lemon juice. Peel, halve, and core the pears and drop them as they are prepared into the bowl. In a large saucepan measure enough water to cover the pears and bring it to a boil with the sugar and orange strips. Add the pears and poach them over low heat for 15 to 20 minutes, or until they are tender. Let the pears cool in the liquid and chill them, covered.

Drain the pears. In a glass bowl combine the cream cheese, honey, salt, lemon juice, and orange rind and blend until smooth. Stir in the dates and chill. Divide the cream cheese filling among the pear halves and garnish the fruit with the almonds. Serve on a bed of salad greens.

NOTE: Canned pear halves, drained, can be substituted for the fresh pears.

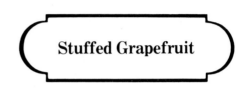

Stuffed Grapefruit

(2 servings)

- 1 grapefruit, halved
- ½ small green pepper, cut into slivers
- ¼ pound sharp Cheddar cheese, grated
- 1 tablespoon salad oil
- Sugar
- 6 leaves Bibb lettuce, rinsed and patted dry

Carefully remove the sections from each grapefruit half, reserving any juice; remove the white membranes, and seed the sections. In a small bowl combine the sections, green pepper, and cheese. In another small bowl combine any reserved juice, the oil, and sugar to taste. Add to the grapefruit mixture and toss gently. Line the grapefruit shells with the lettuce leaves and divide the grapefruit mixture between them.

Vegetable Salads

Vegetable salads are the perfect complement for hearty sandwiches and other entrées. In this section you will find a salad recipe featuring almost any vegetable you can think of, from carrots to beets, from green beans to broccoli, from lentils to chick-peas, from potatoes to soybeans, from artichokes to Brussels sprouts, from zucchini to asparagus. You will find vegetables combined in many-tiered splendors, or elegantly blended, as in W. Peter Prestcott's Simple Trimmed Vegetable Salad. You will see vegetables that have taken center stage—that are not simply healthful and pleasant accompaniments, but sophisticated, satisfying, and imaginative meals.

A few simple tricks can make the preparation of vegetable salads a cinch. An easy way to seed cucumbers is by cutting them in half lengthwise and scooping out the seeds from each half with a small spoon. As we have already noted, tomatoes can be peeled by plunging them whole briefly into boiling water, allowing them to cool, then peeling them. If you prefer vegetables extra crunchy, blanch them briefly by plunging them into rapidly boiling water for a minute or so, then rinse with cool water, and drain well. Green beans, broccoli, and cauliflower are marvelous this way, and the process brings out a wonderful color in vegetables—you will get lovely white cauliflower and spectacularly bright green broccoli or beans.

Wash, trim, and peel vegetables carefully to prepare them properly for salads. You may have to scrub vegetables such as zucchini, which grow close to the soil. You may encounter cucumbers that have been waxed, and you may prefer these scrubbed, too. Cucumbers may also require peeling, as potatoes used for most potato salads do. The bottom portions of broccoli stalks and asparagus, unless garden-fresh, should be scraped with a vegetable peeler to remove the tough outer skins.

24-Karat Salad

(4 servings)

- 4 large carrots, shredded
- ¼ cup salad oil
- ½ tablespoons fresh lemon juice
- ½ teaspoons sugar or honey
- ½ teaspoon salt
- ¼ cup raisins
- ¼ teaspoon celery seed (optional)
- ¼ cup chopped walnuts (optional)

In a bowl combine all the ingredients, except the walnuts, and adjust the seasonings. Let the mixture marinate at room temperature for 1 hour. Just before serving, add the walnuts, if desired, and toss gently.

A SWEET VARIATION: Marinate the raisins in fresh orange juice for 20 minutes and, in addition, substitute fresh orange juice for the lemon juice in the recipe. Drain the raisins and add them to the carrot mixture just before serving.

A LESS SWEET VARIATION: Use fresh lemon juice, as called for in the master recipe and in place of raisins and walnuts use 1 teaspoon chopped parsley and ¼ teaspoon celery seed. Season with freshly ground white pepper to taste.

Green Bean Salad

(4-6 servings)

- 1½ pounds young green beans, trimmed
- ½ pound large white mushrooms
- ½ cup walnut halves
- Salt and freshly ground black pepper
- ¼ cup fresh lemon juice
- ½ cup walnut oil

In a saucepan cook the beans, uncovered, in boiling salted water for 5 to 7 minutes, or until just tender. (They should still be crisp.) Rinse them under cold running water and drain them well. Place the beans in a salad bowl. Cut the mushroom caps and stems into thin julienne strips and add them to the beans with the walnuts and salt and pepper to taste. Add the lemon juice and oil and toss. Let the mixture marinate at room temperature for 1 hour. Serve with assorted cold meats or roasted chicken.

NOTE: Select the beans carefully. The smaller and greener the better, as they are to be used whole.

Walnut oil contributes a rich and nutty flavor to this recipe. It is available at gourmet food stores and better markets.

W. Peter Prestcott's Simple Trimmed Vegetable Salad

(4 servings)

- 1 pound small turnips, peeled and cut into very fine julienne strips
- 1 pound snow peas, trimmed and cut into very fine julienne strips
- 2 small cucumbers, peeled, seeded, and cut into very fine julienne strips
- 1 piece peeled gingerroot (about 1″ square), grated
- 3 tablespoons walnut oil
- 1 tablespoon excellent wine vinegar
- 2 teaspoons dried thyme

Salt and freshly ground black pepper

- ¼ pound chopped walnuts

In a saucepan steam the turnips, snow peas, and cucumber strips for 3 to 5 minutes, being careful not to overcook. Arrange the warm vegetables attractively on a platter and sprinkle the gingerroot over them. In a bowl mix the oil, vinegar, thyme, and salt and pepper to taste and pour over the vegetables. Let cool to room temperature. Sprinkle the walnuts over the vegetables and serve.

Asparagus & Egg Salad

(4 servings)

- 2 pounds asparagus, trimmed of tough ends
- 2 hard-boiled egg whites, finely chopped
- 2 hard-boiled egg yolks, pushed through a sieve
- ½ cup Vinaigrette
- 1 tomato, cut into wedges

Trim the asparagus stalks to a uniform length. In a large skillet cook the asparagus, uncovered, in rapidly boiling salted water to cover until just tender, being careful not to overcook. Remove the stalks with a slotted spoon, rinse them in cold water, and drain thoroughly. Arrange the asparagus on a platter, cover, and chill.

About 1 hour before serving, add the egg whites to the dressing and pour the dressing over the asparagus, leaving the tips undressed. Let the asparagus marinate at room temperature for 1 hour. Just before serving, sprinkle the yolks over the asparagus and garnish the platter with tomato wedges.

Artichoke Hearts Vinaigrette

(3-4 servings)

- 1　14-ounce can artichoke hearts, drained and halved if large
- ½　clove garlic, finely chopped
- ¾　cup Vinaigrette with Herbs
- ¼　cup finely chopped parsley

In a bowl toss artichoke hearts with the garlic and dressing. Let the mixture marinate at room temperature, covered, for 2 to 3 hours. Before serving, sprinkle the salad with parsley and toss again.

Broccoli & Tomato Salad

(4 servings)

- 1　bunch (about ¾ pound) broccoli, cut into flowerets
- 4　ounces blue cheese, crumbled
- ½　teaspoon grated lemon rind
- ¼　cup fresh lemon juice
- ¾　cup salad oil
- 1　teaspoon salt
- 1　cup sour cream
- 3　large tomatoes, cut in wedges
Salad greens

Cook the broccoli in boiling salted water to cover until just tender, about 4 minutes. Drain thoroughly and let cool.

In an enamel or stainless steel bowl combine well the blue cheese, lemon rind, lemon juice, oil, and salt and stir in the sour cream. In a salad bowl pour about ½ of the dressing over the flowerets, toss gently, and chill for 2 to 3 hours. Just before serving, arrange the flowerets and tomato wedges on salad greens on a chilled platter and serve with the remaining dressing.

Ziti Salad with Green Pepper

(4-6 servings)

- 1　green pepper, coarsely chopped
- 1　red pepper, coarsely chopped
- 2　tablespoons chopped scallion, including some of the green tops
- 2　tablespoons finely chopped parsley
- 3　cups cooked ziti pasta, drained and slightly cooled
- ¾　cup Mustard Mayonnaise or Sour Cream Dressing

Combine all the ingredients in a bowl and chill, covered, for 1 hour before serving.

Succulent Cabbage Salad

(4-6 servings)

1-2 oranges, peeled
1 medium head red cabbage, quartered and cored
½ leek, sliced crosswise
Orange juice (optional)

Cut the orange sections into bite size pieces, being careful to reserve the juice. Slice the cabbage thinly. In a salad bowl combine the oranges, cabbage, leek, and juice. Toss lightly and serve. Use orange juice if more dressing is desired.

Beets in Mustard Dressing

(2-4 servings)

1 bunch small to medium beets, trimmed of the greens
1 tablespoon olive oil
1 tablespoon cider vinegar
1 teaspoon Dijon mustard
½ teaspoon dried thyme
½ teaspoon dried basil
Salt and freshly ground black pepper
2 hard-boiled egg yolks, finely chopped

Wash the beets thoroughly, but do not peel them. In a large saucepan cook the beets in boiling salted water to cover for 45 minutes, or until tender. Rinse the beets under cold water, peel them, and cut them into julienne strips. Put the beets in a bowl.

In a small bowl combine the remaining ingredients. Pour the dressing over the beets and let stand for at least 15 minutes before serving. Garnish with the chopped egg yolks.

Onion & Tomato Salad

(4 servings)

4 large tomatoes, peeled and thickly sliced
½ cup chopped red onion
2 tablespoons chopped fresh basil leaves or 2 teaspoons dried
6 tablespoons olive oil
2 tablespoons red-wine vinegar
Salt and freshly ground black pepper

In a bowl sprinkle the tomato slices with the onion and basil. In a small bowl combine the oil, vinegar, and salt and pepper to taste and beat until well blended. Pour over the tomatoes, making sure that all the slices are coated. Let the salad marinate, uncovered, in the refrigerator for 1 to 3 hours.

Mimi Sheraton's Mother's Coleslaw

(4-6 servings)

1 pound green cabbage, shredded
1 small onion, chopped
2 young carrots, chopped
1 small green pepper, chopped
2 teaspoons salt
½ cup distilled white vinegar
2 teaspoons sugar, or as needed
¼ cup corn oil
2 teaspoons dill seeds
White pepper

Combine all the vegetables and chop together until fine and well mixed. In a bowl toss with the salt and let stand for 30 minutes. Pour off any liquid that accumulates. Add the vinegar and toss well but lightly. Let stand for another 20 minutes, tossing once or twice. Drain off excess vinegar. Add the sugar, oil, dill seeds, and pepper and toss lightly but thoroughly. Chill for several hours or overnight. Adjust the seasoning and serve.

Potato Salad

(6 servings)

1½ pounds boiling potatoes, cooked, peeled, and diced
1 hard-boiled egg, finely chopped
¾ cup Mayonnaise
1 tablespoon fresh lemon juice
⅓ cup half-and-half
½ cup finely chopped scallion
½ cup finely chopped sweet pickle
1½ tablespoons finely chopped parsley
1½ teaspoons salt
2 teaspoons snipped fresh dill or ½ teaspoon dried
¼ teaspoon dried marjoram
½ teaspoon dried savory
¼ teaspoon freshly ground black pepper

Put the potatoes in a large bowl and in a small bowl combine well the remaining ingredients. Pour the mixture over the potatoes and toss gently. Chill, covered, until ready to serve.

Potato Salad with Caraway Seed

(4 servings)

1 pound boiling potatoes, cooked, peeled, and diced
½ medium onion, finely chopped
½ cup white-wine vinegar
½ teaspoon caraway seed
½ cup olive oil
1½ tablespoons chopped fresh chives
Salt and freshly ground black pepper

Combine the potatoes and onion in a large bowl. In a small enamel or stainless steel saucepan heat the vinegar and caraway seeds until hot and pour the mixture over the potato mixture. Toss gently. Add the olive oil, chives, and salt and pepper to taste. Toss again. Chill, covered, for several hours before serving.

Richard Sax's Warm Potato Salad with Scallions & Mustard

(6 servings)

2½-3 pounds small red new potatoes scrubbed
Salt
2 teaspoons Dijon mustard
¼ cup red-wine vinegar, or more
Freshly ground black pepper
¾ cup finely minced scallions (use green and white portions)
3-4 tablespoons chopped parsley
½ cup olive oil

In a large saucepan cover the potatoes with cold water by 1 to 2 inches. Bring the water to a boil, add a large pinch of salt, and boil the potatoes until tender, about 15 minutes. Do not overcook. Drain the potatoes.

In a small bowl toss together the mustard, vinegar, and several grinds of pepper. If desired, peel the potatoes with a paring knife and slice them back into the pan in which they cooked. Alternatively, cut them into bite-size wedges. Add the scallions and mustard mixture and toss lightly. Add the parsley, olive oil, and a little salt and toss again. Correct the seasonings with more vinegar, salt, or pepper, as needed. Serve warm.

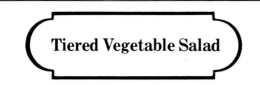

Tiered Vegetable Salad

(12 servings)

1   head iceberg lettuce, shredded
1   large red onion, finely chopped
1   8-ounce can water chestnuts, drained and sliced
2   green peppers, chopped
5   stalks celery, thinly sliced
1¼ cups fresh peas, blanched, or 1 10-ounce package frozen small peas, partially thawed
2   cups Mayonnaise
½   cup freshly grated Parmesan or Romano cheese
4   medium tomatoes, peeled and seeded
1   cup fresh lemon juice
4   strips bacon
1   bunch watercress leaves, chopped
12 pitted black olives, quartered and chilled
3   hard-boiled eggs, quartered

The day before serving, cover the bottom of a large glass salad bowl or soufflé dish with a layer of shredded lettuce. Top with a layer of onion, a layer of water chestnuts, a layer of peppers, a layer of celery, and a layer of peas. Cover the final layer with mayonnaise and sprinkle it with the grated cheese. Cover tightly and refrigerate. Cut the tomatoes into julienne strips and in a bowl combine them with the lemon juice. Cover and refrigerate.

One hour before serving, in a small skillet sauté bacon until crisp, turning it frequently. Drain the bacon on paper towels and crumble it. Sprinkle the watercress and bacon over the salad. Drain the tomatoes and arrange them on top with the olives and quartered hard-boiled eggs. To serve, cut through the layers with a large spoon.

WITH HAM & CHEESE: A layer of boiled ham or Swiss cheese or both, thinly sliced, may also be added.

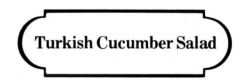

Turkish Cucumber Salad

(6 servings)

4   cups plain yogurt
1   tablespoon olive oil
3-4 medium cucumbers, peeled, seeded, and cut into ¼-inch slices
1   clove garlic, finely chopped
2   tablespoons finely chopped mint leaves
Salt
Mint sprigs

In a large bowl whisk the oil slowly into the yogurt until well combined, add the cucumbers, garlic, mint leaves, and salt to taste, and mix gently. Chill for at least 2 hours before serving. Garnish with mint sprigs.

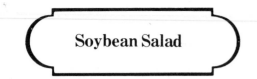

Soybean Salad

(6 servings)

1 pound dried soybeans
2 teaspoons salt
¾ cup diced red pepper
¾ cup diced green pepper
½ cup olive oil
1 clove garlic, finely chopped
1 tablespoon ground cumin
1 teaspoon finely chopped canned green chili
2 cups sliced scallions, including some of the green tops
½ pound feta cheese, cut into ½-inch cubes
¼ cup chopped pitted black olives
1 tablespoon fresh lemon juice
¼ cup finely chopped parsley
Freshly ground black pepper

Soak the soybeans overnight in cold water to cover. Drain them, discarding the liquid, and put them in a large saucepan with water to cover. Add the salt, bring the water to a boil, and simmer the mixture, partially covered, for 3 hours, or until the beans are tender. Drain.

In a large skillet sauté the peppers in the oil over moderately high heat for 5 minutes, add the garlic, cumin, and chili, and sauté the mixture for 3 minutes. Add the scallion and toss until just softened. Stir in the soybeans and cook until heated through. Add the cheese and olives and stir gently for 3 to 4 minutes, or until the cheese softens slightly. Transfer the mixture to a heatproof bowl, add the lemon juice, parsley, and pepper to taste, and serve at room temperature.

Michael Batterberry's Fresh Tomato & Celery Salad

(4 servings)

1 generous pint box cherry tomatoes (about 38-44), peeled
1½ teaspoons sugar
1 teaspoon coarse salt
4 tender inner stalks celery, thinly sliced
1½ tablespoons cumin
3 tablespoons peanut or salad oil
Juice of 1 lime
Salt and freshly ground white pepper

Sprinkle the tomatoes with sugar and coarse salt and let stand for 1 hour. Scatter cumin over a piece of foil and roast in a medium oven (350° F.) for a few minutes. When spice begins to darken remove instantly as it scorches easily. Drain tomatoes and toss them in a bowl with cumin and celery. Beat oil and lime juice together and pour over the salad. Toss and add salt and pepper to taste.

Zucchini & Rice Salad

(6 servings)

5 tablespoons olive oil
4 medium zucchini, coarsely chopped
1 medium onion, finely chopped
2 cloves garlic, finely chopped
1½ cups cold cooked rice
1 cup chopped parsley
6-8 fresh basil leaves, finely chopped, or
½ teaspoon dried
½ cup chopped walnuts
¼ cup freshly grated Parmesan cheese
Juice of ½ lemon
1 teaspoon salt
Freshly ground black pepper

In a skillet sauté the zucchini in 2 tablespoons of the oil for 5 minutes, add the onion and garlic, and cook for 15 minutes. Transfer the mixture to a large heatproof bowl, add the rice, parsley, basil, and walnuts, and toss. Let the salad cool, and refrigerate.

Thirty minutes before serving, sprinkle the salad with the remaining oil, Parmesan cheese, lemon juice, and salt and pepper to taste. Toss and adjust seasonings.

Rice & Artichoke Salad

(6 servings)

1½ cups uncooked rice
3¾ cups Chicken Stock or canned
chicken broth
½ cup Mayonnaise
½ cup sour cream
¾ teaspoon curry powder
½ green pepper, chopped
½ red pepper, chopped
4 scallions, thinly sliced
1 14-ounce can artichoke bottoms,
drained and chopped
25 pimiento-stuffed olives, sliced
1 14-ounce can artichoke hearts,
drained

In a saucepan cook the rice in the chicken stock for 20 minutes, or until tender, and let it cool.

In a large bowl combine well the rice, mayonnaise, sour cream, and curry powder. Add the remaining ingredients, except the artichoke hearts, and toss. Before serving, garnish the salad with the artichoke hearts.

Seafood, Meat & Poultry Salads

These are substantial salads, and certain to satisfy. Within the wide variety presented here you will find new ways with familiar dishes. Leftovers enter a new dimension as the basis for one of these attractive salads. Yesterday's chicken was never so welcome as a creative opportunity; choose from the many salads in this section. And there are recipes for beef and lamb as well, and even duck.

When preparing leftover meat and poultry for use in salads, consider the texture you'll want in the finished dish. Slice or sliver chicken for a chef's salad, but you will want good-sized chunks for other salad recipes. Make sure all meat and poultry is trimmed of gristle.

Canned tuna is the base for two of these recipes. Use tuna packed in oil for its superior texture and flavor, but drain it well before adding it to other ingredients.

The other seafood salads in this section must be prepared with the freshest of ingredients. Shellfish is expensive, but a little goes a long way. Two cups of shrimp or crab meat are ample for four servings of several of these seafood salads, and two pounds of shrimp will be enough for six to eight servings of Shrimp and Rice Salad.

Extra care must be taken in the proper preparation of seafood and shellfish. Pick over cooked crab meat carefully to find and remove all bits of cartilage. If a recipe calls for boiled shrimp, you can save some work by shelling them after they have been boiled, rinsed in cool water, and drained. You will find it much easier than handling them raw. And be mindful not to overcook them. Boil shrimp for a very short time—you will see them begin to turn pink after a couple of minutes. Once pink, rinse with cold water to cool them quickly, or they will toughen almost immediately. If you are readying mussels, begin by rinsing them in several changes of cold water. Scrub the shells vigorously with a brush, and remove their beards—the black fibers that protrude from between the shells. You needn't cover them with water if they are to be steamed; a cup or two at the bottom of the pot will do nicely. When the shells open, the mussels are cooked. Always remember when preparing any shellfish that those that remain unopened after cooking should be discarded.

Some of these recipes call for prepared dressings, while others include the bases for dressings (such as oil and vinegar) in the overall list of ingredients. Remember to use a light touch when dressing, or you may overpower the main ingredients.

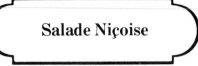

Salade Niçoise

(6 servings)

3 cups cooked green beans, cut into 1-inch lengths
3 tomatoes, quartered
1¼ cups Vinaigrette
3 cups sliced cooked boiling potatoes
1 head Boston lettuce
½ cup pitted black olives
3 hard-boiled eggs, quartered
12 canned flat anchovy fillets
1 7-ounce can oil-packed tuna, drained and flaked
1 tablespoon finely chopped parsley
1 tablespoon finely chopped fresh basil or 1½ teaspoons dried

In a bowl combine the beans and tomatoes with ¼ cup of the dressing. In another bowl let the potatoes marinate in ¼ cup of the dressing for 30 minutes. Toss the lettuce leaves in ¼ cup of the dressing and arrange them around the sides of a large salad bowl. Put the potatoes in the middle of the bowl and surround them with the beans and tomatoes, olives, eggs, and anchovies. Arrange the tuna on top. Pour the remaining dressing over the salad, sprinkle with parsley and basil, and serve.

Shrimp & Rice Salad

(6-8 servings)

2 pounds large shrimp
2¼ cups uncooked rice
½ cup heavy cream
1 cup Mayonnaise
1 red pepper, finely chopped
1 green pepper, finely chopped
1-2 cups Green Mayonnaise

Place the shrimp in a large saucepan in 4 cups boiling salted water and cook them for about 3 minutes, or until they turn pink. Do not overcook. Drain, reserving the cooking liquid, shell and devein the shrimp, and let them cool at room temperature.

In the saucepan bring 2¼ cups of the reserved liquid to a rapid boil, add the rice, and stir once. Cover, reduce the heat to the lowest possible flame and cook, without stirring, for 20 minutes. Cool.

In a bowl combine well the cream and mayonnaise, add the peppers and rice, and toss. Put the rice mixture on a serving platter and arrange the shrimp around the rice. Serve with green mayonnaise.

NOTE: To shell and devein the shrimp, remove the shell and rinse the shrimp under cold running water. With a small sharp knife cut a ⅛-inch slit along the outside curve of the shrimp, exposing a blackish vein. With the knife tip lift out the vein and rinse the shrimp again.

Basic Shellfish Salad

(4 servings)

 2 cups cooked small shrimp, or picked-over and flaked crab meat, or lobster meat, in chunks
 1 cup Mayonnaise, Green Mayonnaise, or Russian Dressing
 Salad greens
 Garnishes

In a bowl combine the shellfish with the dressing. (You may prefer to stir in only a portion of the dressing and serve what remains in a separate bowl.) On a chilled platter arrange the shellfish salad on a bed of greens and garnish the platter with any of the following: capers, olives, hard-boiled eggs, cucumber slices, green pepper rings, pimientos, chilled cooked asparagus, tomato wedges, chopped parsley, chopped fresh chives.

Tuna & Bean Salad

(4 servings)

 1 cup dried white beans or kidney beans
 2 cups Chicken Stock or canned chicken broth
 ⅓ cup olive oil
 ¼ cup red-wine vinegar
 Salt and freshly ground black pepper
 1 red onion, thinly sliced
 1 7-ounce can oil-packed tuna, drained and flaked
 Finely chopped parsley

Soak the beans overnight in cold water to cover. Drain the beans, discarding the liquid, and put them in a large saucepan. Add the chicken stock or broth, bring the liquid to a boil, and simmer the mixture, partially covered, for 1 to 1 ½ hours, or until the beans are tender. Drain the beans and transfer them to a serving bowl. Toss the beans with the olive oil and vinegar. Season with salt and pepper to taste and let the beans marinate at room temperature for 1 hour.

Add the onion slices and tuna and toss. Before serving, if desired, drizzle the beans with additional olive oil and vinegar to taste and garnish them with the parsley.

Crab Ravigote

(4 servings)

1 teaspoon Dijon mustard
1 teaspoon finely chopped parsley
1 hard-boiled egg, finely chopped
3 tablespoons cider vinegar
1 tablespoon olive oil
1 teaspoon salt
Cayenne
2 cups picked over and flaked cooked crab meat
1½-2 cups Green Mayonnaise

In a bowl combine well all the ingredients, except the crab meat and mayonnaise, and season to taste with the salt and cayenne. Add the crab meat and toss. Spoon the mixture into scallop shells or divide it among plates and garnish each serving with some mayonnaise. Serve the remaining mayonnaise in a bowl on the side.

Mussels with Mustard Mayonnaise

(6 servings)

1 quart mussels, well washed and scrubbed, with beards removed
½ cup dry white wine
½ cup Mayonnaise
½ cup heavy cream
1 teaspoon Dijon mustard
1 tablespoon finely chopped parsley
1 tablespoon finely chopped fresh chives
1 tablespoon finely chopped fresh tarragon or 1½ teaspoons dried
Chopped parsley
Lettuce leaves (optional)
Very thin slices of raw beet (optional)

In a large pot cook the mussels in the wine over high heat, covered with a tight-fitting lid, for about 5 minutes, or until the shells open. Discard any mussels that do not open. Let the mussels cool and remove them from the shells, reserving half of the shells.

In a bowl combine well the mayonnaise, cream, mustard, and herbs. Add the mussels and toss them with the dressing. Put the mussels back in the half- shells, top each shell with a dollop of dressing, and garnish with the beets and some of the parsley. Or serve the salad on lettuce leaves on a chilled platter and garnish with the parsley.

Shellfish & Melon Salad

(4 servings)

¼ cup heavy cream
½ ounce Scotch whisky
Pinch curry powder
1 cup Mayonnaise
1 cup drained 1-inch melon cubes
   (honeydew, casaba, or Spanish melon)
2 cups cooked small shrimp, or picked
   over and flaked crab meat, or lobster
   meat, in chunks
Lettuce leaves
Paprika

In a bowl combine the cream, whisky, curry powder, and mayonnaise, and mix until smooth. Stir in the melon and shellfish gently. On a chilled platter arrange the salad on a bed of lettuce leaves and garnish it with a sprinkling of paprika.

Marinated Beef Chanticleer

(4 servings)

¾ pound cold cooked roast beef, cut
   into julienne strips
1 medium onion, grated
3 tablespoons fresh lemon juice
1¼ cups sour cream
1½ tablespoons Dijon mustard
1 small clove garlic, crushed
Salt and freshly ground white pepper
Lettuce leaves
Tomato slices

In a large bowl combine the beef, onion, and 1¼ tablespoons of the lemon juice. In another bowl combine well the sour cream, remaining lemon juice, mustard, garlic, and salt and pepper to taste. Adjust the seasonings as desired. Pour the sour cream mixture over the beef, toss, and chill for several hours. Serve on a bed of lettuce garnished with tomato slices.

Minted Lamb Salad

Macaroni & Meat Salad

(4 servings)

2 cups thinly sliced cold roast lamb
2 cups sliced cooked boiling potatoes
Salt
1 tablespoon chopped fresh mint
½-¾ cup Vinaigrette
Lettuce leaves
Mint sprigs

In a bowl combine the lamb and potatoes and add salt to taste. In a small bowl add the mint to the dressing and pour the dressing over the lamb mixture. Let the salad marinate at room temperature for 1 hour. Drain it and serve on a bed of lettuce on a platter garnished with mint sprigs.

(6 servings)

3 cups diced cooked cold lamb, veal, or chicken
3 cups cooked cold macaroni
1 tablespoon chopped onion
½ cup chopped celery
¼ cup chopped pimiento-stuffed green olives
1 sour pickle, chopped
Salt and freshly ground black pepper
1 cup Mayonnaise
Lettuce leaves

In a bowl combine the meat or poultry and macaroni. In another bowl combine the onion, celery, olives, and pickle and add to the meat or poultry mixture. Season to taste. Add the mayonnaise and toss gently. Chill, covered, for 1 hour and serve on a bed of lettuce leaves.

Pork & Rice Salad

(4 servings)

1½ tablespoons Dijon mustard
1 teaspoon salt
2 tablespoons fresh lemon juice
2 tablespoons fresh orange juice
½ cup olive oil
Hot pepper sauce
2½ cups julienne strips cold cooked pork
¼ cup finely chopped parsley
3 cups cold cooked rice
2-3 oranges, in sections
1 small red onion, thinly sliced
Watercress

In a large bowl combine well the mustard, salt, lemon juice, and orange juice. Add the oil and beat vigorously. Add the hot pepper sauce to taste and pour the mixture over the pork. Let the mixture marinate at room temperature for 30 minutes. Add the parsley and rice, mix, and adjust the seasonings. Refrigerate, covered, for several hours, or overnight.

Combine the orange sections and onions with the pork mixture. Toss gently, arrange on a platter, and chill. Remove the salad from the refrigerator about 1 hour before serving. Garnish with watercress.

Ham & Grapefruit Salad

(6 servings)

3 grapefruits, in sections
2 avocados, peeled and sliced
¾ pound cold cooked ham, cut into julienne strips
¾ cup finely chopped celery
3 tablespoons fresh lemon juice
3 tablespoons olive oil
Salt and freshly ground white pepper
6 tablespoons sour cream
1 cup Mayonnaise
Lettuce leaves

In a ceramic or glass bowl combine the grapefruit sections, avocados, ham, celery, lemon juice, oil, and salt and pepper to taste, and toss gently. Let the mixture marinate in the refrigerator for 30 minutes.

In a small bowl combine the sour cream and mayonnaise and blend until smooth. Add half the mayonnaise mixture to the grapefruit mixture and toss. Serve the salad on a bed of lettuce leaves and pass the remaining dressing in a separate bowl.

Chef's Salad

Chicken Salad Español

(6 servings)

6 cups combined salad greens, such as Boston lettuce, romaine, iceberg lettuce, escarole, watercress
1 cucumber, peeled, seeded, and sliced
3 scallions, including some of the green tops, chopped
2 cups each of julienne strips of cold cooked ham or tongue, and chicken or turkey
¾ pound Swiss cheese, cut into julienne strips
3 hard-boiled eggs, quartered
3 tomatoes, cut into wedges
12 pitted black olives
1½ cups Garlic Vinaigrette

In a large salad bowl combine the salad greens, cucumber, and scallions and toss. Arrange the ham or tongue and poultry and cheese on top. Arrange the eggs, tomatoes, and olives decoratively on top. Serve the dressing separately in a sauceboat.

(4 servings)

½ cup Mayonnaise
¼ cup plain yogurt
1 teaspoon fresh lemon juice
2 tablespoons chili sauce
2-3 drops hot pepper sauce
Salt and freshly ground white pepper
1½ cups cold cooked chicken, in chunks
1 stalk celery, thinly sliced (optional)
Lettuce leaves
1 green pepper, thinly sliced into rings
5 pimiento-stuffed green olives
5 pitted black olives
1 small onion, thinly sliced and separated into rings
2 tomatoes, cut into wedges
2 hard-boiled eggs, halved

In a large bowl combine the mayonnaise, yogurt, lemon juice, chili sauce, hot pepper sauce, and salt and pepper to taste, and blend until smooth. Add the chicken and celery, if desired, and toss. Serve the salad on a bed of lettuce leaves, and surround the chicken with green pepper, olives, onion rings, tomatoes, and eggs.

W. Peter Prestcott's Chicken Salad

(8-10 servings)

2 large sweet red peppers
1 stalk celery with leaves, chopped
1 carrot, coarsely chopped
½ onion, sliced
4-6 sprigs parsley
1 bay leaf
5 cups water
3 whole chicken breasts (about 2½ pounds), skinned and boned
½ cup olive oil
3 tablespoons red-wine vinegar
1¼ cups (4 ounces) chopped walnuts
1 bunch scallions, including some of the green tops, thinly sliced
1 tablespoon dried tarragon, crumbled
½ pound medium-small mushrooms, quartered
2 pounds medium-sized new potatoes
½ cup dry white wine
4 anchovy fillets, rinsed and finely chopped
½ cup Calamata olives, slivered, *or* ¼ cup pitted, slivered oil-cured black olives
1½ teaspoons salt
¼ teaspoon freshly ground black pepper
2 tablespoons lemon juice, or more to taste
Leaf lettuce

Place the red peppers directly on the gas burners of your stove, at high heat (or as close to the broiling element as possible, if you don't have a gas stove). Keep turning them until the skin has blackened all over. Cool them for 4 to 5 minutes. Place the peppers in a plastic bag, close it, and let stand for 15 to 20 minutes.

In a large saucepan combine the celery, carrot, onion, parsley, bay leaf, and water. Bring to a boil, cover, and simmer for 10 minutes. Add the chicken and poach for 10 minutes, or until barely cooked. Remove the chicken to a cutting board, reserving the stock.

Remove the peppers from the bag, halve them lengthwise, and remove the seeds, stems, and ribs. Scrape off all the black skins with a knife. Cut each half of the roasted peppers into 8 lengthwise strips. Halve the strips if they are long. Cut the chicken into 3-inch strips ¼ to ½ inch thick. Toss with the oil, vinegar, walnuts, scallions, peppers, and tarragon.

Strain the stock and in a pot heat it to simmering. Add the mushrooms and simmer 2 minutes. Drain the mushrooms and add them to the chicken. (Save the stock for another use.)

Drop potatoes into boiling water and boil until just tender, 15 to 20 minutes. Peel, cut into ½-inch cubes, and in a bowl combine them while warm with the wine. Let stand until the wine is absorbed, tossing twice.

Add the potatoes to the chicken. Add anchovies, olives, salt, pepper, and 2 tablespoons lemon juice (or more, if desired). Toss gently. Let stand at least 30 minutes and serve in a shallow bowl lined with the lettuce.

Curried Chicken & Shrimp Salad

(4-6 servings)

½ cup Mayonnaise
¾ cup sour cream
1 tablespoon Dijon mustard
1 teaspoon curry powder
1 clove garlic, finely chopped
1½ cups cold cooked rice
Dry white wine, *or* water
¾ cup cold cooked chicken, in chunks
½ pound cold cooked shrimp, shelled and deveined (optional)
1 10-ounce package frozen peas, partially thawed
1 red pepper, cut into julienne strips
½ cup sliced leek (white part only)
2 small endives, separated into leaves

In a bowl combine the mayonnaise, sour cream, mustard, curry powder and garlic and blend thoroughly. Add the rice, toss, and add a little white wine or water to thin the mixture if necessary. Add the chicken, shrimp, peas, red pepper, and leek. Toss gently and adjust the seasonings. Transfer the salad to a bowl lined with endive leaves.

Duck & Orange Salad

(4 servings)

3 cups julienne strips lean cold roast duck
1 small Bermuda onion, thinly sliced
3 tablespoons fresh lemon juice
¼ teaspoon salt
Freshly ground black pepper
6 tablespoons olive oil
¼ teaspoon dry mustard
Rind of 1 orange, grated
1 tablespoon butter
1 small clove garlic, crushed
¼ cup coarsely chopped walnuts
3 medium oranges, peeled, thinly sliced crosswise, and seeded
Salt

In a large bowl combine the duck and onion. In another bowl combine the lemon juice, salt, pepper to taste, oil, mustard, and orange rind and blend thoroughly. Pour over the duck, cover, and let marinate, stirring occasionally, in the refrigerator for 2 hours.

In a small skillet heat the butter, add the garlic, and cook until golden. Add the walnuts and cook, stirring, until they are lightly browned. Remove the garlic.

Add the orange slices to the duck mixture, toss, and season with additional salt. Garnish with nuts and serve.

Molded Salads

The salads in this section all share one enormously attractive attribute: they need only minimal last-minute fussing— unmolding and garnishing, perhaps—and can be prepared in advance. You can relax with your guests until minutes before your molded salad is to be served, and enjoy your own party as much as your guests do.

Molded salads can be a visual treat, thanks to the variety of beautiful and fanciful molds now available in department stores and gourmet shops. Since the jellied liquid in a molded salad is transparent, the salad ingredients will be visible and should be arranged in an esthetically pleasing manner. This is a challenge you may well enjoy.

The first step in a molded salad is to dissolve the gelatin in a hot liquid (water, juice, or broth). The gelatin will thicken to a consistency that will bind the salad's heavier ingredients. Be very careful; too much gelatin will "toughen" a salad. Follow directions, and these salads will be firm, but not overly so.

The preparation of molded salads can require a bit of time. Gelatin needs to be partially set so that the other ingredients that are to be added to it do not sink to the bottom of the mold. It may take anywhere from twenty minutes to an hour before your gelatin will be firm enough for you to proceed to the next step in the recipe. Check on its progress occasionally as it chills, and once it begins to thicken you can proceed.

To unmold one of these salads is not nearly as difficult as it may seem. Oil your mold lightly before you fill it. When your salad is firm (a final chilling time of at least several hours is suggested), simply dip the bottom of the mold into hot water for four to five seconds, run a thin knife around the inside rim, invert a plate over the mold, turn the mold and plate upside down, and tap to unmold the salad onto the plate.

Molded salads encompass a remarkable variety, from Helen Witty's Remolded Broccoli Salad to Crown of Shrimp in Aspic and Caviar Ring, from Molded Spinach or Gazpacho Salad to Grapefruit Ring or Fruit and Cottage Cheese Mold. Here are molded salads for luncheon, to serve as accompaniments to heartier fare, or to prepare a selection of several for an unusual and appealing Salad Bar Buffet.

Molded spinach salad

Helen Witty's
Remolded Broccoli
Salad

(6 servings)

2   pounds broccoli, or more, if the stems are thick, separated into flowerets and trimmed

6   quarts boiling water

Salt

⅓   cup strained fresh lemon juice, or to taste

1-2 teaspoons Dijon mustard

Salt

Freshly ground white pepper

1   cup virgin olive oil

3   tablespoons capers, drained

3   tablespoons diced bottled pimientos

¼   cup sliced stuffed green olives

2   tablespoons minced parsley

About 4 anchovy fillets, rinsed, patted dry, and halved lengthwise

6   slender strips bottled pimientos

Additional sliced stuffed olives for garnish (optional)

Parsley (optional)

Rinse and drain the broccoli flowerets and split (from the stem end upward) any that are much larger than the rest.

Bring the water to a boil in a large pot and add a handful of salt. When it boils again drop in the broccoli, return to a boil, and cook, uncovered, just until tender-crisp, about 8 to 10 minutes. Do not overcook. Set the pot under the tap and run cold water into it until the broccoli is no longer warm. Cool.

Place the largest broccoli floweret, stem up, in the center of a 5- to 6-cup bowl, such as a stainless steel mixing bowl. Pack more flowerets around it, stems toward the center, until the sides of the bowl are lined. Fill in the center with any remaining pieces. With a small plate press gently but firmly to pack the broccoli together. (At this point, the broccoli may be refrigerated, covered, for up to several hours.)

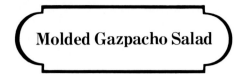

Molded Gazpacho Salad

(4-6 servings)

1   tablespoon unflavored gelatin
1⅔ cups cold tomato juice or V-8 juice
2   tablespoons red-wine vinegar
1   large tomato, peeled, seeded, and chopped
1   cucumber, peeled, seeded, and chopped
¼   cup chopped scallions
¼   teaspoon freshly ground black pepper
¾   teaspoon salt
1   teaspoon sugar
1   clove garlic, finely chopped
Watercress

In a small bowl let the gelatin soften in ¼ cup of the juice for 3 to 5 minutes. In a saucepan heat the remaining juice over low heat and stir in the gelatin. Stir until the gelatin dissolves completely. Remove the pan from the heat and add the remaining ingredients, except the watercress, combine well, and pour into a lightly oiled 1-quart mold. Chill, covered, until firm. Unmold the salad and serve it on a platter garnished with watercress.

Molded Spinach Salad

(6 servings)

3   10-ounce packages frozen chopped spinach, thawed and drained
2½ cups sour cream
¼   cup chopped celery
3   tablespoons chopped onion
1   tablespoon cider vinegar
1   tablespoon chopped parsley
½   teaspoon dried tarragon
½   teaspoon dried chervil
Salt and freshly ground black pepper
¼   cup peeled, seeded, and chopped cucumber

In a bowl combine well the spinach, ½ cup of the sour cream, and the remaining ingredients, except the cucumber, and pour into a lightly oiled 1½-quart ring mold. Chill, covered, until firm.

In a bowl combine the remaining sour cream with the cucumber and mix until blended. Unmold the salad onto a platter, and fill the center with some of the cucumber dressing. Serve the remaining dressing in a separate bowl.

Fish Mousse with Mustard Cucumber Dressing

(6 servings)

2 pounds flounder fillets or other fillets of white fish

3 cups white fish stock, *or* bottled clam juice

Bouquet garni: 1 bay leaf, 2 branches fresh thyme or ½ teaspoon dried, 4 sprigs parsley

2 tablespoons unflavored gelatin

4 tablespoons dry white wine

¾ cup heavy cream, chilled

1½ teaspoons dried dill

¼ teaspoon salt

Freshly ground white pepper

1 cucumber, peeled, seeded, and grated

1 cup Mayonnaise

1 tablespoon Dijon mustard

1 tablespoon fresh lemon juice

Watercress leaves

In a stainless steel or enamel saucepan or skillet combine the fish, stock or clam juice, and bouquet garni. (The liquid should cover the fillets.) Bring the liquid to a boil and simmer the mixture, covered, for 10 minutes, or until the fish is just tender. Strain, reserving the liquid and discarding the bouquet garni. Flake the fish.

In a saucepan let the gelatin soften in the wine for 3 to 5 minutes. Over low heat stir in 2 cups of the reserved cooking liquid and stir the mixture until the gelatin dissolves completely. Do not let it boil. In a blender or food processor blend the mixture with the fish for 1 to 2 minutes. Pour the mixture into a bowl and chill until it is partially set.

In a chilled bowl whip the cream lightly and fold it into the fish mixture. Add the dill, salt, and pepper to taste and adjust the seasonings. Pour into a lightly oiled 1½ quart ring mold or fish-shaped mold. Chill, covered, until firm.

In a bowl combine the cucumber, mayonnaise, mustard, and lemon juice and blend thoroughly. Before serving, unmold the mousse, garnish it with watercress leaves, and serve it with the cucumber dressing.

(Preceding pages) Fish mousse with mustard cucumber dressing

Seafood & Rice Ring

(6 servings)

- 1 tablespoon unflavored gelatin
- ¼ cup cold water
- ¾ cup cooked rice
- 1 pound cooked peas
- ¼ cup cider vinegar
- ¾ teaspoon salt
- Freshly ground white pepper
- ¼ teaspoon paprika
- 1 teaspoon sugar
- ¾ cup salad oil
- ½ cup shelled and deveined chopped cooked shrimp
- ½ cup picked over and flaked cooked crab meat
- ½ cup chopped steamed mussels (see page 59)
- ¾ cup Mayonnaise
- ¼ pound shelled and deveined whole cooked shrimp (optional)

In a small heatproof bowl let the gelatin soften in the cold water for 3 to 5 minutes. Put the bowl in a pan of simmering water and stir the gelatin until it dissolves completely. In a large bowl combine the rice and peas. In a bowl combine well the vinegar, salt, pepper to taste, paprika, sugar, and oil. Stir the gelatin and vinegar mixtures into the rice mixture and toss lightly. Pack into a lightly oiled 1½-quart ring mold and chill, covered, until firm.

In a bowl combine the chopped shrimp, crab meat, mussels, and mayonnaise, tossing gently.

Before serving, unmold the ring on a platter and fill the center with the seafood salad. Garnish the top of the ring with the whole shrimp, if desired.

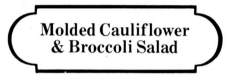

Molded Cauliflower & Broccoli Salad

(8 servings)

- 1 large cauliflower, cut into flowerets
- 1 large broccoli, cut into flowerets
- Salt
- ¾ cup Vinaigrette
- ¼ cup chopped parsley
- 1 hard-boiled egg, chopped
- 1½ cups Curry Mayonnaise

In a saucepan blanch the cauliflower and broccoli flowerets in boiling salted water to cover for 5 minutes, or until just tender. Rinse under cold running water and drain well.

Fill a 1½- or 2-quart bowl to the rim with alternate layers of cauliflower and broccoli. Pour the dressing over the vegetables and press down lightly with a plate. Refrigerate 2 to 3 hours. Just before serving, unmold gently and sprinkle with parsley and chopped egg. Serve with a bowl of curry mayonnaise on the side.

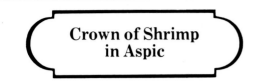

Crown of Shrimp in Aspic

(6 servings)

1½ tablespoons unflavored gelatin
½ cup dry white wine
3 cups hot White Fish Stock, *or* canned chicken broth
Few drops fresh lemon juice
2 egg whites, beaten until frothy
4-5 ripe tomatoes, peeled, seeded, and quartered
½ pound cooked shrimp, shelled and deveined
Watercress
2 cups Mayonnaise, flavored with a little tomato paste, or tomato juice

In a small bowl let the gelatin soften in the wine for 3 to 5 minutes. In a saucepan heat the stock or broth over low heat until hot, add the gelatin, and stir until it is completely dissolved. Add the lemon juice and egg whites and bring to a boil, whisking constantly. Remove the pan from the heat without disturbing the mixture and let it stand for 5 minutes. Bring the mixture to a boil again, whisking, remove it from the heat, and let it stand for 5 minutes. Repeat the process one more time. Strain the mixture through a double layer of cheesecloth into a bowl and let it cool. (The mixture must remain liquid. If it starts to thicken, heat it slightly over low heat.)

Cover the bottom of a lightly oiled 1-quart mold with a layer of aspic and chill until partially set. Arrange the tomato quarters, rounded sides down, in the aspic and cover with aspic. Chill until partially set. Arrange some of the shrimp on the aspic and chill. Continue to fill the mold, alternating layers of aspic and shrimp, chilling the mold each time a layer of aspic is added. Chill, covered, until firm.

Before serving, unmold the salad and fill the center of the ring with watercress. Serve with the tomato-flavored mayonnaise.

Caviar Ring

(6 servings)

1   tablespoon unflavored gelatin
½ cup cold milk
1   cup Mayonnaise
1   tablespoon fresh lemon juice
1   cup heavy cream, whipped
1   tablespoon finely chopped onion
1   cup black lumpfish caviar
Salad greens
2   cups Shellfish Salad

In a saucepan let the gelatin soften in the milk for 3 to 5 minutes. Stir the mixture over low heat until the gelatin dissolves completely. Let the mixture cool and stir in the mayonnaise, lemon juice, whipped cream, onion, and caviar. Pour into a lightly oiled 1-quart ring mold and chill until firm.

Before serving, unmold the salad on a platter of greens and fill the center with shellfish salad.

NOTE: This is a good first course or luncheon dish. Use a fish-shaped mold, omit the greens and shellfish salad, and serve with crackers as a cocktail spread.

Salmon Mold

(6 servings)

⅓ cup fresh lemon juice
⅔ cup cold water
2   tablespoons unflavored gelatin
1   16-ounce can salmon, picked over and flaked in its liquid
1   cup peeled, seeded, and finely chopped cucumber
½ cup chopped green pepper
1   4-ounce jar pimientos, drained and chopped
1   tablespoon finely chopped onion
1   cup Mayonnaise
1   cup evaporated milk
Salt
Sliced cucumber

In a measuring cup let the gelatin soften in the lemon juice and cold water for 3 to 5 minutes. Put the cup in a pan of simmering water and stir the gelatin until it dissolves completely. Pour into a bowl and let cool. Add the salmon, cucumber, green pepper, pimientos, and onion and mix well. Stir in the mayonnaise and milk and season with salt to taste. Pour into a well-oiled 1½-quart fish-shaped mold and chill, covered, until firm.

Before serving, unmold and garnish with the cucumber slices arranged on the top of the salad to resemble the scales of a fish.

Tuna Ring

(4-6 servings)

1 tablespoon unflavored gelatin
¼ cup cold water
2 7-ounce cans tuna, drained and flaked
½ cup Herb Mayonnaise
1 tablespoon finely chopped onion
1 tablespoon fresh lemon juice
Salt and freshly ground black pepper
1 cup sour cream
Lettuce leaves
Chopped parsley or fresh dill
Drained pimientos

In a measuring cup let the gelatin soften in the water for 3 to 5 minutes. Put the cup in a pan of simmering water and stir it until the gelatin dissolves completely. Let the gelatin cool. In a blender or food processor blend the tuna, mayonnaise, onion, lemon juice, and salt and pepper to taste until smooth. In a bowl combine the tuna mixture, sour cream, and gelatin and spoon into a lightly oiled 1-quart mold. Chill, covered, until firm. Before serving, unmold onto a platter lined with lettuce leaves and garnish with parsley or dill and pimientos.

Tomato & Ham Aspic

(4 servings)

2 tablespoons unflavored gelatin
½ cup cold water
2 cups tomato juice
2 teaspoons Worcestershire sauce
½ teaspoon salt
¼ teaspon freshly ground black pepper
1 apple, peeled, cored, and diced
6 ounces boiled ham, diced
Lettuce leaves

In a small bowl let the gelatin soften in the water. In a saucepan heat the tomato juice over low heat, add the gelatin and stir to dissolve. Add the Worcestershire sauce, salt, and pepper and stir. Chill until partially set. Fold in the apple and ham. Spoon the mixture into 4 lightly oiled ½-cup molds and chill until firm. Before serving, line salad plates with lettuce leaves and unmold each salad onto a plate.

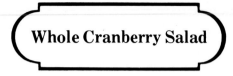

Whole Cranberry Salad

(6 servings)

1 tablespoon unflavored gelatin
¾ cup cold water
3 cups picked over and rinsed cranberries
2 cups sugar
1 cup fresh orange juice
Salad greens

In a small bowl let the gelatin soften in ¼ cup of the water. In a saucepan combine 2 cups of the cranberries with the remaining water and cook, covered, over moderate heat for about 15 minutes, or until the skins pop. Force berries with the liquid through a sieve into a saucepan and add the sugar, orange juice, and the remaining cup of cranberries. Bring the mixture to a boil and simmer it over low heat for 5 minutes. Add the gelatin and stir gently until it dissolves. Remove the pan from the heat and remove the whole berries with a slotted spoon. Arrange the berries in the bottom of a lightly oiled 1-quart mold, pour in enough of the berry liquid to just cover them, and chill until partially set. Add the remaining liquid and chill, covered, until firm.

Before serving, unmold on a platter and garnish with salad greens.

Fruit & Wine Salad Mold

(4 servings)

1 cup fresh fruit, such as bananas and oranges and grapefruit, peeled, pith and white membranes removed
1 3-ounce package lemon-flavored gelatin
1 cup boiling water
½ cup dry white wine
½ cup fruit juice, *or* water
½ cup halved seedless grapes
½ cup heavy cream, whipped

Dice the fruit and reserve the juices from the orange or grapefruit. In a heatproof bowl let the gelatin dissolve in the water. Cool, and stir in the wine and fruit juice or water. Pour one third of the gelatin mixture into a 1-quart mold, add the grapes, and chill until partially set. Top the grapes with a layer of fruit, add one third more gelatin mixture, and chill until partially set.

Chill the remaining gelatin mixture until partially set and fold in the whipped cream. Top the mold with the cream mixture and chill until firm. Before serving, unmold onto a platter.

NOTE: Fresh pineapple can be used in gelatin only if it is first boiled for 2 minutes.

Grapefruit Ring

(8 servings)

2 3-ounce packages lemon-flavored gelatin
1½ cups boiling water
⅓ cup frozen lemonade concentrate
2 cups cold water
2 grapefruits, in sections
1 cup halved and seeded red grapes
½ cup chopped celery
2 cups creamed cottage cheese
Celery leaves

In a heatproof bowl let the gelatin soften in 1½ cups boiling water until it dissolves. Stir in the lemonade concentrate and 2 cups cold water and chill until partially set. Fold in grapefruit sections, then the grapes and celery. Spoon into a lightly oiled 1½-quart ring mold and chill, covered, until firm.

Before serving, unmold, fill the center with cottage cheese, and garnish the mold with celery leaves.

Fruit & Cottage Cheese Mold

(4-6 servings)

1 tablespoon unflavored gelatin
3 tablespoons canned pineapple juice
3½ cups creamed cottage cheese
1 cup Mayonnaise
½ tablespoon grated lemon rind
2 teaspoons celery seed
1 cup lemon yogurt
Salt
Salad greens
Sliced pineapple
Strawberries

In a small heatproof bowl let the gelatin soften in the pineapple juice for 3 to 5 minutes. Put the bowl into a pan of simmering water and stir the gelatin over low heat until it dissolves completely. Combine the cottage cheese and gelatin and spoon the mixture into a lightly oiled 1-quart mold or divide it among 6 individual molds. Chill, covered, until firm.

In a bowl combine well the mayonnaise, lemon rind, celery seed, yogurt, and salt to taste. Chill the dressing, covered.

Before serving, unmold the salad onto a platter lined with salad greens. Garnish with pineapple slices and strawberries and serve with the dressing.

Fruit Salads

There are endless possibilities for fruit salads: oranges, grapefruits, tangerines, apples, grapes, cherries, peaches, pears, plums of all shades, papayas, pineapples, a profusion of melons, strawberries, blueberries, fragile raspberries and blackberries, bananas. Wonderful surprises, such as kiwi fruit, honey tangerines, and fresh mandarin oranges, have recently arrived on the American scene. Combine them to your heart's delight in an endless series of surely satisfying experiments.

Here you will find fruit salads as you know and love them, with some new variations on familiar themes. Banana Split Salad is a dish so appealing most desserts pale by comparison. Here also are exciting and unusual fruit salads, guaranteed to expand the range of even the most creative practitioner of the culinary arts. Try Avocado Citrus Salad for a new twist on orange and grapefruit salads; consider combining grapes with nuts, or slices of cucumber; raise oranges to a new level with Michael Batterberry's Sherried Orange Salad (it includes translucently thin slices of sweet red onion).

For the best possible fruit salad, choose fruits that are in season; you will get the best for less. Select all fruits with care to avoid bruises or flaws. Firm apples will be crisp; cherries and grapes should have deep color; melons should be heavy and slightly fragrant; ripe pears, peaches, and plums will yield slightly to the touch as will ripe oranges and grapefruit, pineapple and papaya. Buy only ripe berries—those that are deep in color—for they will not mature once picked.

If fruits are your passion, invest in a covered bowl designed specifically to ripen them (available in department and gourmet stores). An assortment of fruits will ripen more successfully than any number of one specific fruit. Many fruits will ripen in a day or two inside a closed brown paper bag, but this is not a foolproof method, so do not depend on it.

Most fruits cannot be prepared in advance, for once cut they will soften and discolor. A sprinkling of lemon or lime juice will keep cut pears or apples white for a short time, though. Wash and pick over berries just before serving. They will become soft if stored moist. Citrus fruits are an exception. Peel and section them when you have time, and store them in their own juice in a closed container in the refrigerator.

Almost all fruit salads are easy to prepare. Plan on them, relax, and enjoy the compliments they are sure to bring.

Sweet Slaw

(4-6 servings)

- 1   5-¼-ounce can crushed unsweetened pineapple with juice
- ½   cup Mayonnaise
- 4   ounces raisins
- 1   medium head cabbage (about 1 pound), quartered, cored, and finely shredded

Drain the pineapple, reserving the juice. In a small bowl thin the mayonnaise with some of the reserved juice to the consistency of heavy cream. In a bowl combine the pineapple, raisins, and mayonnaise mixture and blend thoroughly. Let the mixture marinate, covered, in the refrigerator overnight. Before serving, add the cabbage and toss.

CURRIED VARIATION: Substitute 1 12-ounce can pears, diced, for the pineapple and 1 tablespoon chutney for the raisins. Thin the Mayonnaise with pear syrup to taste and stir in 2 teaspoons, or more to taste, curry powder.

Avocado Citrus Salad

(4 servings)

- ¼   cup sugar
- 1   teaspoon salt
- 1   teaspoon paprika
- 1   teaspoon Dijon mustard
- ⅓   cup fresh lime juice
- ⅔   cup salad oil
- Lettuce leaves
- 3   oranges, in sections
- 2   grapefruits, in sections
- 1-2   avocados
- Fresh lime juice

In a blender or food processor blend the sugar, salt, paprika, mustard, lime juice, and salad oil for 20 seconds.

Peel the avocados, slice them, and brush the slices lightly with lime juice. Arrange the orange and grapefruit sections alternately with the avocado slices on individual chilled salad plates lined with lettuce leaves. Put a dollop of the dressing on each salad and serve the remaining dressing in a bowl.

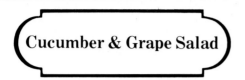

Cucumber & Grape Salad

(2-4 servings)

2 cucumbers, peeled, seeded, and diced
1 teaspoon salt
1 cup plain yogurt
1 clove garlic, finely chopped
1 tablespoon white vinegar
½ teaspoon salt
⅛ teaspoon freshly ground white pepper
1 scallion, finely chopped
3 mint leaves, chopped
1 cup seedless green grapes
Romaine lettuce
Mint

In a colander sprinkle the cucumbers with the salt and let them stand for 5 minutes. Rinse under cold running water and dry on paper towels.

In a salad bowl combine the yogurt, garlic, vinegar, salt, pepper, scallion, and mint. Add the cucumbers and grapes and toss gently. Chill, covered, for at least 1 hour. Serve on a bed of romaine lettuce and garnish with mint sprigs.

Grape & Nut Salad

(6 servings)

½ pound grapes, halved and seeded
2 pears, peeled, cored, and cut into wedges
1 small grapefruit, in sections
½ cup grapefruit juice, preferably fresh
2 tablespoons white rum
¾ cup walnut halves

In a bowl combine the grapes, pears, grapefruit, and grapefruit juice. Sprinkle with rum and garnish with the nuts. Chill the salad for about 15 minutes in the refrigerator before serving.

Michael Batterberry's Sherried Orange Salad

(8-12 servings)

- 2 medium red onions, sliced as thinly as possible
- 8 navel oranges, peeled, all pith and white membranes removed
- ¼ cup honey (3 generous tablespoons), plus ½ tablespoon
- ½ cup Amontillado sherry
- ¼ cup fresh lemon juice
- Coarse salt and freshly ground white pepper
- ½ cup salad oil
- 3 tablespoons white-wine or rice vinegar
- Salad greens

Put the onions in a strainer over a bowl and leave under cold running water for at least 10 minutes. (Or soak in bowl of cold water for 1 hour or so, changing water 5 or 6 times.) Place the orange sections in a bowl. In a cup dissolve the honey in ¼ cup sherry and the lemon juice, pour over the oranges, and let marinate for 1 hour or more in the refrigerator. Dry the onions with paper towels, season with salt and white pepper, and let marinate in remaining sherry for 1 hour. In the blender blend at high speed the oil, vinegar, ⅓ cup liquid from the oranges, ½ tablespoon honey, and 3 tablespoons of the onion sherry. Season with salt and white pepper. On a platter lined with salad greens arrange the oranges and onions, drained. Just before serving, toss with the dressing.

Fruit & Cottage Cheese Platter

(6 servings)

- Romaine lettuce
- 2 cups small curd cottage cheese
- 3 grapefruit, in sections
- 5 oranges, in sections
- 3 tangerines, in sections
- ½ pineapple, pared, cored, and cut into spears
- 2 apples, peeled, cored, sliced lengthwise, and sprinkled with lemon juice
- Nuts (optional)
- Coconut (optional)
- Avocado or Cinnamon Yogurt Dressing

Line a serving platter with romaine lettuce and place the cottage cheese in the center. Arrange the fruit decoratively around the cheese. If desired, sprinkle the fruit with nuts and coconut. Serve with a bowl of dressing.

NOTE: Fruit platters should be kept, covered, in the refrigerator until ready to serve.

(Preceding pages) Banana split salad

BLUE CHEESE VARIATION: Combine 1 cup cottage cheese with 4 ounces blue cheese and ¼ cup sour cream and mix thoroughly. Chill for about 15 minutes. On a platter surround the cheese with apple wedges, pear wedges, seedless grapes, and strawberries, all sprinkled with fresh lemon juice. Garnish with mint leaves.

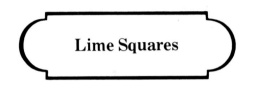

Lime Squares

(6-8 servings)

2   3-ounce packages lime gelatin
2   cups boiling water
1¼ cup cold water
1   teaspoon fresh lemon juice
1   8-ounce package cream cheese, softened
1   cup fresh fruit, such as peeled diced peaches, cored diced pears, seedless grapes, or sliced strawberries
Lettuce leaves

In a heatproof bowl dissolve the gelatin in 2 cups boiling water. To ½ cup of the cold water, stir in ½ cup of gelatin mixture and set aside. Add the remaining ¾ cup cold water and the lemon juice to the large bowl and stir. Blend in the cream cheese until smooth. Chill until partially set.

Fold fruit gently into the gelatin mixture, spoon it into an 8-inch square pan, and chill until firm. Top with the reserved set lime gelatin. Chill for several hours. Before serving, cut into squares and arrange on a platter lined with lettuce leaves, or on individual serving plates lined with lettuce leaves.

Banana Split Salad

(4 servings)

Lettuce leaves
2   bananas, peeled, halved lengthwise, and brushed with fresh lemon juice
½   orange, in sections
1   cup diced fresh fruit, such as seedless grapes, peaches, plums, strawberries, and so on
½   cup heavy cream, whipped
Chopped nuts

Line 4 chilled salad plates with lettuce and put half a banana on each plate. Top the banana with some of the orange sections and fresh fruit. Garnish each serving with a dollop of whipped cream and sprinkle with nuts.

Pineapple & Bean Salad

(6 servings)

1 14-ounce can pineapple chunks, juice
  reserved
1 1-pound can red kidney beans,
  drained and rinsed
1 10-ounce package frozen lima beans
1 10-ounce package frozen cut green
  beans
1 green pepper, chopped
1 cup sliced celery
1 tablespoon cornstarch
¼ cup wine vinegar
1 tablespoon Dijon mustard
½ teaspoon freshly ground black pepper
2 teaspoons fresh snipped dill or ½
  teaspoon dried
2 teaspoons sugar
1 teaspoon salt
¼ cup olive oil

In a large bowl combine the pineapple and kidney beans. In a saucepan cook the lima beans and green beans in boiling salted water until just tender. Drain, refresh under cold running water, drain again, and add to the pineapple mixture. Add the green pepper and celery, cover, and chill for several hours.

In a small enamel or stainless steel saucepan blend ½ cup of the reserved pineapple juice with the cornstarch. Add the vinegar, mustard, pepper, dill, sugar, and salt and stir over moderate heat until thickened. Remove the pan from the heat and slowly beat in the olive oil. Cover and chill.

One hour before serving, combine the dressing with the pineapple-bean mixture and let stand at room temperature, uncovered, until ready to serve.

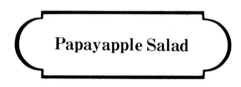

Papayapple Salad

(4-6 servings)

2 cups peeled, seeded, and diced
  papaya
2 cups pared, cored, and diced
  pineapple
¼ cup pineapple juice
¼ cup fresh lime juice
Lettuce leaves
Flaked coconut
1-2 cups Sour Cream and Honey
  Dressing

In a bowl combine the papaya, pineapple, and juices, and toss. Chill, covered, for at least 1 hour. Arrange on a platter with lettuce leaves and garnish with coconut. Serve the dressing separately in a bowl.

The Salad Bar Buffet

A salad presents possibilities. A salad bar presents even more, and the options to be had at a salad bar buffet are really almost endless. It is a perfect way to feed and entertain a large number of people and requires only a little effort in preparation and presentation. Once arranged and made ready, the salad bar virtually takes care of itself. To be sure, the salads may have to be replenished, but this kind of attention does not compare with bending over a hot stove waiting for a casserole to finish baking. Also, the salad bar is a healthful alternative to other, often rich buffet offerings.

Center your buffet around a large green salad, and provide a profusion of accompaniments to please any number of guests. Fresh produce can be made into natural and colorful arrangements. Try alternating colors and textures. Place bowls of black olives alongside bowls of thin rings of green peppers. Have carrot curls on hand, raw cauliflower or broccoli flowerets, sliced cooked beets, marinated or raw mushrooms, red pepper slices, scallion brushes, drained pimientos, sliced avocados dipped in lemon juice to prevent discoloring, bean sprouts, sliced cucumbers and turnips, asparagus spears, marinated green beans, marinated artichoke hearts and hearts of palm.

Don't limit your table to produce. Consider chopped nuts, such as pecans or walnuts; slices of cheese or bowls of creamed cottage cheese or yogurt; crisp crumbled bacon; sliced hard-boiled eggs; bean curd; chick-peas; raisins and other dried fruits; orange and grapefruit sections, and fresh fruits such as grapes and berries. And croutons are a must.

As your choice of salad and accompaniments is varied, so should your dressings be. Any of the recipes in this book would serve well at a salad bar buffet. Just make sure that you have enough on hand. Make your dressings ahead of time and keep them in covered containers in the refrigerator. Bring them to room temperature before serving.

For a truly sumptuous buffet, choose a few substantial salads you can make somewhat ahead of time to round out the offerings on your table. Molded salads would be perfect, or salads of meat and/or poultry with pasta or rice. Or, prepare a tureen of a splendid rich soup to accompany a green salad bar.

As a finishing touch for a truly memorable buffet, have on hand some interesting rolls and a selection of breads. Cuban White Bread, sourdough rye, and some other breads from the Sandwich section would be ideal.

Sandwiches

Ever since the mid-eighteenth century, when John Montagu, the Fourth Earl of Sandwich—clearly more passionate about gambling than food—slapped cold beef between two slices of bread rather than leave the gaming table, sandwiches have been immensely popular for their simplicity and convenience. Indeed, the imprimatur of the Earl immediately made sandwiches fashionable—as teatime delicacies, with aristocratic ladies presenting them as dainty morsels on fine china, as well as hearty meals-on-the-go.

There was, and is, good reason for the sandwich's universal popularity. Certainly sandwiches are the easiest meal to make, serve, and eat. They can be simple or slightly or extravagantly fancy; they can be tiny bites or mouth stretchers; fairly light or real stick-to-the-ribs. They are served for breakfast, for lunch, for dinner, for Sunday supper, at tea, with cocktails, on picnics, in bed at midnight. What other class of food has such versatility or lends itself to so much improvisation?

A good sandwich begins with good bread, and the baker's sampler we offer includes a chewy Cuban White Bread, a hearty rye and a wholesome wheat, an herb bread and a crunchy Apple Walnut loaf. Next come the fillips, the appetizing extras that can transform the most mundane sandwich into a memorable repast: Flavored Butters, a variety of Mayonnaises, Russian Dressing, homemade Honeyed Ketchup, Coleslaw, pickles, and relishes.

Of course, every household in America has its favorite sandwich combination. But how about slipping a sandwich made with homemade Cashew Butter into the lunchbag instead of plain old Peanut Butter. Or adding apples and cucumbers to your favorite Tuna Fish Salad, or curry and ginger to Egg Salad. Or mixing horseradish with cream cheese to spread on a salami sandwich. Or making spicy Lamb Burgers. How about serving an open-faced sandwich, a sauced sandwich, a rolled sandwich. Make a sandwich a three-course meal. Make a smørrebrød, taco takeouts, or pita platters. Make a party or a picnic. A sandwich lends itself to any occasion.

A poor boy sandwich, with garnishes.

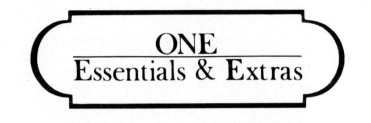

ONE
Essentials & Extras

Breads

Bread. What's the magic that changes so simple a combination as flour and water into something so splendid? It's the yeast, of course, that makes the dough rise, and gives it flavor and texture. There's no trick to yeast, though, no mystery—just chemistry.

Yeast is alive but not active in its dried form. To activate, put the yeast in a bowl and add warm water. Some recipes also call for a small amount of sugar (the amount will vary from recipe to recipe as it affects the final flavor and texture of the bread). This is to stimulate the action of the yeast. The water should feel warm to your fingers and warm to your wrist. (Too warm water will kill the yeast. To err on the cool side will slow the yeast down, but won't do any harm.) Stir a couple of times, if you like, to help the yeast dissolve. You should begin to see bubbles and foaminess and some thickening of the mixture in less than 10 minutes. What you're doing here, besides liquefying the yeast, is proving that it's alive.

Once you've proofed the yeast, you're ready to make bread. As you mix in the flour, water, and whatever other ingredients the recipe calls for, the activated yeast begins to feed on the starch in the flour and multiply. Also, as you mix, the gluten molecules in the flour become moistened and "gluey" and begin to stick together, forming a stretchy network throughout the dough.

Kneading smooths the dough and develops its elasticity. Push the dough out, fold it back on itself, give it a quarter turn, push out again: you are working so that all the gluten molecules will be moistened. As you handle the dough you'll be able to feel the stretchiness. Push the dough out; it will pull back on its own. This is the smooth, elastic dough that most bread recipes describe—dough ready for rising.

The crucial time in breadmaking is the rising. The yeast are still feeding and multiplying, creating by their activity bubbles of gas that push up against the net of gluten and cause the dough to rise. As rising continues, the gluten ripens—and the flavor and texture of the dough develops. It is a slow process. You must wait until the dough has doubled in volume.

How do you know when the dough has doubled in volume? It will have a swollen look about it—higher in the middle—and feel flabby or spongy to the touch. Stick a finger about an inch into the center of the dough. If the dent remains, the dough has doubled in volume and you can punch it down. It's almost ready for baking.

But what if you punched down the pita before it quite doubled in volume? What if you put the herb dough in too warm a spot and it rose very quickly? What if you didn't quite get the knack of the kneading? Well, you won't have an absolutely perfect loaf of bread, but it will still taste delicious.

Breads: Cuban white, country wheat, Swedish-style rye, apple walnut

Cuban White Bread

(2 loaves)

4	packages active dry yeast
2½	cups warm water
1	tablespoon sugar
5½-7	cups unsifted all-purpose flour
1	tablespoon salt
¼-½	cup cornmeal

Proof the yeast by placing it in a small bowl and stirring in 1½ cups of the warm water and the sugar. Set the bowl aside until the mixture begins to bubble and foam, about 5 minutes.

Place 5½ cups of the flour in a large bowl and make a well in the center. Pour in the proofed yeast mixture, the remaining cup of warm water, and the salt. Stir with a wooden spoon until the ingredients are well combined, then transfer to a floured board. Knead, incorporating more flour as you proceed, until you have a smooth, elastic, and fairly stiff dough. Gather the dough into a ball and place it in a lightly greased bowl. Cover with a damp towel and set aside in a warm, draft-free place until the dough has doubled in volume, about 1 hour.

Punch the dough down with a blow of your fist, remove it from the bowl, and cut it in half. Shape each half into a mound. Sprinkle a large baking sheet with the cornmeal and set the loaves well apart on the sheet. With a sharp knife, cut several slashes across the top of each loaf. Place the baking sheet in the center of a cold oven.

Turn the heat on to 350°and bake for 1 hour, or until the loaves sound hollow when tapped with your finger. Cool on wire racks.

NOTE: This recipe results in a delicious, crusty, French-like bread, but one that will not keep longer than a day or two at the most. Like other breads, though, it takes well to freezing.

Hot Dog & Hamburger Rolls

(16 rolls)

Follow the Cuban white bread recipe up to the point where you remove the dough from the bowl after you have punched it down. Instead of cutting the dough in half, roll it out to ½″ thick. For hot dog rolls, cut out rectangles of dough approximately 3″ x 5″. For hamburger rolls, cut circles out of the dough—about 3″ in diameter. Place 2″ apart on a lightly greased large baking sheet and let rest for half an hour. Then brush with melted butter and set in a cold oven. Turn the temperature to 350° and bake for 1 hour, or until the rolls sound hollow when tapped with your finger. Cool on wire racks.

English Muffins

(16 muffins)

Follow the Cuban white bread recipe up to the point where you remove the dough from the bowl after you have punched it down. For English muffins, instead of cutting the dough in half, roll it out on cornmeal to ½″ thick and cut out 3″ circles. Let the circles of dough rest for 15 minutes, then place several at a time (as many as can fit comfortably) in a lightly greased skillet over medium heat and cook for 10 to 15 minutes, turning two or three times as they brown.

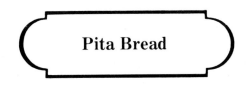

Pita Bread

(8 pitas)

1	package active dry yeast
¾	teaspoon sugar
½	cup warm water
1½-2½	cups sifted all-purpose flour
¾	cup warm water
3	tablespoons vegetable oil

Proof the yeast by placing it in a large bowl and stirring in the sugar and ½ cup warm water. Set the bowl aside until the mixture begins to bubble and foam, about 10 minutes.

Add 1 cup of the flour to the yeast mixture and gradually stir in the ¾ cup warm water. Add the oil, then the remaining flour, a half cup at a time, stirring with a wooden spoon until the ingredients are well combined. The dough should be soft but not sticky. Transfer to a well-floured board and knead until you have a smooth, elastic dough. Gather the dough into a ball and place in a lightly greased bowl. Cover with a damp towel and set aside in a warm, draft-free place until the dough has doubled in volume, about 1 hour.

Punch the dough down with a blow of your fist, cover it again with a damp towel, and allow to rest for half an hour.

Shape the dough into an 8″ long roll and cut the roll into 8 equal parts. Make the 8 pieces of dough into 8 balls, then flatten each very thin with the palm of your hand. They should be circular in shape, about 6½″ in diameter. Put the pitas on floured baking sheets, four to a sheet, and let stand at room temperature for 1 hour. Preheat the oven to 500°.

Bake the pitas on the floor of the oven, one baking sheet at a time, for 5 minutes each at 500°. Cool on wire racks.

To keep pitas moist, cover with plastic wrap or store in plastic bags. To make a pocket to stuff with fillings, cut a 3″ slit along the edge of each pita and pry the bread apart gently.

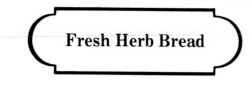

Fresh Herb Bread

(2 loaves)

1	package active dry yeast
1½	cups warm water
3	tablespoons sugar
½	cup milk, scalded
2	teaspoons salt
5	tablespoons butter, softened
5½-6½	cups sifted all-purpose flour
½	cup finely chopped fresh chives
½	cup finely chopped parsley
½	cup finely chopped fresh dill
3	tablespoons finely chopped fresh chervil or 1 tablespoon dried

Proof the yeast by placing it in a small bowl and stirring in the warm water and 1 tablespoon of the sugar. Set the bowl aside until the mixture begins to bubble and foam, about 10 minutes.

Combine the hot milk, remaining 2 tablespoons of sugar, salt, and 3 tablespoons of the butter in a large bowl. Stir with a wooden spoon until well blended. Cool to lukewarm, then stir in the proofed yeast mixture. Gradually stir in 3 cups of the flour and add the herbs. Beat as vigorously as you can until the mixture is smooth, then transfer to a floured board. Knead, incorporating as much of the additional flour as you need to make a stiff dough. Gather the dough into a ball and place it in a lightly greased bowl. Cover the bowl with a damp towel and set aside in a warm, draft-free place until it has doubled in volume, 1 to 2 hours.

Punch the dough down with a blow of your fist and let it rest 15 minutes. Then remove the dough from the bowl and cut it in half. Set each half into a lightly greased 9 x 5 x 3″ loaf pan. Preheat the oven to 375°.

Melt the remaining 2 tablespoons butter and brush the loaves lightly. Cover each with a damp towel and set aside to double again in volume, about 1 hour.

Bake in the center of the oven for 30 minutes, or until the bread sounds hollow when tapped with your finger. Cool on wire racks.

TEA SANDWICH VARIATION: Prepare the herb bread dough as described above, but do not mix in the herbs. After the dough has doubled in volume, been punched down, and rested 15 minutes, divide it in half and follow the directions below:
1. On a lightly floured surface, roll each half into an 8 x 11″ rectangle. *2.* Brush each rectangle with melted butter. Combine herbs and sprinkle evenly over dough. With the short side facing you, roll up each rectangle and tuck the ends in securely. *3.* Set each loaf into a lightly greased 9 x 5 x 3″ loaf pan. Cover with a damp towel and set aside to double in volume, about 1 hour. Preheat the oven to 375°. *4.* Bake for 20 to 30 minutes. Cool on wire racks. When sliced, the herbs will appear in a spiral pattern.

Preparation of herb bread

1.

2.

3.

4.

Swedish-style Rye Bread

(3 loaves)

1	package active dry yeast
½	cup warm water
2	teaspoons sugar
2	cups rye flour
2	cups boiling water
¾	cup molasses
6	tablespoons butter, softened
1	tablespoon salt
6-7	cups unsifted unbleached white flour
1	egg white, lightly beaten
1	teaspoon caraway seed
1	teaspoon poppy seed

Proof the yeast by placing it in a small bowl and stirring in the warm water and the sugar. Set the bowl aside until the mixture begins to bubble and foam, about 10 minutes.

Place the rye flour in a large bowl and make a well in the center. Pour in the boiling water, then add the molasses, butter, and salt. Stir with a wooden spoon until the ingredients are well combined. Cool to lukewarm, then stir in the proofed yeast mixture. Transfer to a floured board. Gradually incorporate up to 7 cups of the white flour and knead until you have a smooth, elastic dough. Gather the dough into a ball and place in a lightly greased bowl. Cover with a damp towel and set aside in a warm, draft-free place until the dough has doubled in volume, about 2 hours.

Punch the dough down with a blow of your fist. Cover the bowl with a damp towel and set aside to rise again, this time for about 20 minutes.

Knead again briefly and divide the dough into 3 equal balls. Shape each into a round loaf.

Grease a large baking sheet and set the loaves well apart on the sheet. Cover with a damp towel and set aside to double in volume, about 1 hour. Preheat the oven to 350°.

Brush each loaf with the beaten egg white and sprinkle with the caraway and poppy seeds. Bake in the center of the oven for 40 to 50 minutes, or until the bread sounds hollow when tapped with your finger. Cool on wire racks.

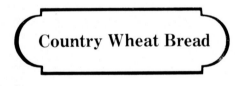

Country Wheat Bread

(1 loaf)

1	package active dry yeast
1½	cups whole wheat flour
1	tablespoon light brown sugar
1½	cups warm water
3	cups whole wheat flour
3	tablespoons butter, softened
2	tablespoons light brown sugar
1	tablespoon salt
¼-½	cup warm water

Place the yeast in a large bowl, add the 1½ cups of whole wheat flour and the tablespoon of brown sugar, and stir in the 1½ cups of warm water. Cover the bowl with a towel and set aside in a warm place for 8 to 12 hours (at least 8 hours). This is the starter (the yeast is proofed in the process).

To make the bread, add the 3 cups of whole wheat flour, the butter, brown sugar, and salt to the bowl of starter. Stir with a wooden spoon until the ingredients are well combined, adding up to ½ cup of warm water to keep the dough mixable. It should be very stiff.

Take out about a cup of this stiff dough, cover well, and refrigerate or freeze. This will be the starter for your next loaf. Transfer the remaining dough to a floured board. Knead until you have a smooth, elastic dough. Gather the dough into a ball and place in a lightly greased bowl. Put the bowl in a pan of warm water, cover it with a damp towel, and set aside in a warm, draft-free place until the dough has doubled in volume, about 2 hours.

Punch the dough down with a blow of your fist, cover again, and set back to rise for another 1 to 1½ hours. Preheat the oven to 450°.

When the dough has risen the second time, put it into a greased and floured 9 x 5 x 3″ loaf pan. Bake for 20 minutes at 450°, then turn the oven down to 300° and bake for 40 minutes more, or until the bread sounds hollow when tapped with your finger. Cool on wire racks.

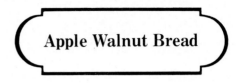

Apple Walnut Bread

(1 loaf)

4	tablespoons butter, softened
⅔	cup sugar
2	eggs, beaten
2	cups sifted all-purpose flour
1	teaspoon baking powder
1	teaspoon baking soda
1	teaspoon salt
2-3	Cortland or other cooking apples (2 cups), peeled, cored, and finely chopped
⅔	cup coarsely chopped walnuts
1	tablespoon grated lemon peel

Preheat the oven to 350°.

Cream the butter with the sugar until light and fluffy. Then beat in the eggs.

Sift together the flour, baking powder, baking soda, and salt, and add alternately with the chopped apples to the creamed butter mixture. When the ingredients are well combined, stir in the nuts and the lemon peel.

Spread the batter into a lightly greased 9 x 5 x 3″ loaf pan and bake in the center of the oven for 45 to 55 minutes, or until a toothpick inserted into the center of the bread comes out clean and dry. Cool on a wire rack.

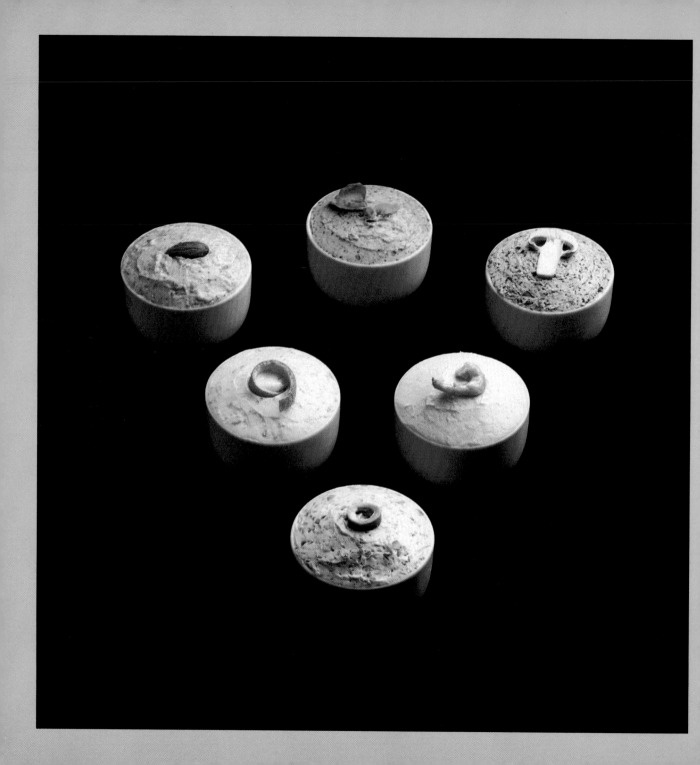

Spreads

Be it butter, mayonnaise, ketchup, or mustard, most people smooth a spread on their bread before they slap on the filling for a sandwich. Butter is probably the usual—plain butter. But to make a simple sandwich splendid, consider flavored butters. Garlic Butter is an obvious one: try it on a sliced chicken sandwich. Or try that sliced chicken with Herb Butter, ham on rye with mustard butter, hamburgers with Mushroom Butter. Or have a bread and olive butter sandwich.

If it's mayonnaise you like, you'll love it homemade. Whip up a jarful in no time. You can use your electric mixer or blender—or food processor, if you have one. The master recipe is easy and makes a very out-of-the-ordinary mayonnaise. From there, proceed to the variations: green, with herbs; tangy, from curry or anchovies or onions; Russian, as in the dressing.

For ketchup enthusiasts, we offer a honey-flavored variety that you'll really want to spread around. Wait till you taste it on a scrambled eggs sandwich!

Say "mustard" and most people think of the ball park variety—a mild, bright yellow seasoning so many of us have been slathering on hot dogs and ham sandwiches since childhood. But there's a whole world of mustards out there, hundreds of them, and they can really spice up a sandwich nicely.

Basically, prepared mustard is a blend of mustard seeds (white or yellow and/or black or brown), salt, spices, and vinegar. There are smooth mustards and grainy ones. The grainy ones contain whole or crushed seeds to add texture (these tend to be regarded with suspicion by children). There are mild mustards and spicier ones. They're all good on frankfurters, but a perfect pairing of mustards and meats can be spectacular. Try Grey Poupon (a mild mustard) on cold chicken, Gulden's Spicy Brown on roast beef, Polish-style Kosciusko on meat loaf or ham. Zatarain's Creole mustard, a mildly spicy, grainy mustard is terrific on leftover lamb; so is Dijon on cheese-on-rye. Very hot Chinese and Japanese mustards would be wonderful with leftover pork, as would mild, sweet Düsseldorf and Bavarian mustards.

Flavored butters: almond, watercress, mushroom, smoked salmon, olive, orange

Flavored Butters

(½ cup)

Take ¼ pound (1 stick) unsalted butter and put it in a bowl. When it has softened a bit, cream the butter by mashing it against the sides of the bowl with a wooden spoon until it is light and fluffy. To make one of the flavored butters listed below, add the appropriate ingredients to the bowl of creamed butter and blend well.

The butters can be refrigerated in tightly covered containers for up to 2 weeks. Or, shape them into a cylinder on a sheet of waxed paper, roll up tightly, and freeze, cutting off just as much as you need each time.

ANCHOVY BUTTER: Add 1 tablespoon anchovy paste; 1 tablespoon finely chopped fresh chives; 1 tablespoon capers, drained and finely chopped.

ALMOND BUTTER: Add ¼ cup almonds, finely ground, and ½ teaspoon salt.

BLUE CHEESE BUTTER: Add ½ pound (1 cup) blue cheese, crumbled, and 2 teaspoons fresh lemon juice.

GARLIC BUTTER: Add 1 small clove garlic, crushed.

HERB BUTTER: Add 1 tablespoon each finely chopped parsley, fresh basil, and fresh chives.

MUSHROOM BUTTER: Add ½ pound mushrooms, sliced, sautéed in 2 tablespoons butter and then finely chopped; 1 teaspoon salt; and 2 tablespoons dry sherry.

OLIVE BUTTER: Add 2 tablespoons green pitted olives, finely chopped, and 2 teaspoons fresh lemon juice.

ORANGE BUTTER: Add 2 teaspoons grated orange rind plus 1 teaspoon orange juice.

WATERCRESS BUTTER: Add ½ bunch watercress (leaves only), minced; 1 tablespoon lemon juice; 1 teaspoon salt; and freshly ground black pepper to taste.

SMOKED SALMON BUTTER: Add ¼ pound smoked salmon, finely chopped, and freshly ground black pepper to taste.

Mayonnaises

The master recipe for Mayonnaise can be found on page 110 of the salad section. What follows are delicious variations on the theme.

MUSTARD MAYONNAISE: In a chilled bowl lightly whip ⅔ cup heavy cream. Combine 1½ cups Mayonnaise, 4 tablespoons fresh lemon juice, and 3 tablespoons Dijon mustard until well blended. Fold in the cream and add salt to taste.

ANCHOVY MAYONNAISE: Into 1 cup of Mayonnaise blend 2 tablespoons anchovy paste, ¼ cup finely chopped parsley, and 2 teaspoons capers, drained and finely chopped.

ONION MAYONNAISE: For every 1 cup of Mayonnaise, add 1 tablespoon grated onion, ¼ teaspoon Worcestershire sauce, and salt and freshly ground white pepper to taste. Refrigerate for at least 3 hours before using. Adjust seasonings if necessary.

GREEN MAYONNAISE: Blend into 1 cup of Mayonnaise ¼ cup finely chopped spinach leaves, 1 tablespoon each finely chopped parsley, fresh tarragon, and fresh chives. (Depending on the availability of fresh herbs and your own taste, you may substitute—or add—fresh mint, chervil, dill, or watercress.)

RUSSIAN DRESSING: Finely chop ½ tablespoon each green and red peppers, 2 teaspoons fresh chives, and 4 tablespoons sour dill pickle (if you like a sharp flavor to your dressing). Place in a small bowl with 1 cup of Mayonnaise and ½ cup chili sauce. Stir until the ingredients are well combined.

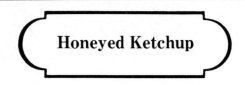

Honeyed Ketchup

(2 cups)

1 quart canned tomato purée
1 cup cider vinegar
½ cup honey
1 teaspoon salt
1 teaspoon dry mustard
1 cinnamon stick
1 teaspoon whole allspice or
   1 teaspoon powdered
4 small onions, left whole

Combine the tomato purée, vinegar, honey, salt, and mustard in a 2- to 3-quart enamel-iron casserole or stainless steel pot and bring to a boil. Meanwhile, wrap the cinnamon stick and allspice in a small piece of cheesecloth and tie with string to make a bag. Add this and the onions to the casserole and bring the mixture back to a boil. Adjust the heat so that the ketchup barely simmers and cook uncovered for 3 hours. Stir frequently to prevent the ketchup from sticking to the bottom of the pan. Remove the onions and spice bag and pour the hot ketchup into a heated glass jar equipped with a tight-fitting lid. Cool to room temperature, then refrigerate.

Pickles & Relishes

Crispy pickles and perky relishes are perfect accompaniments for so many sandwiches. Homemade, they're extra special. The recipes in this chapter are not at all difficult, but there are some important things to know about packing and sealing:

Canning jars are ideal containers for the pickle and relish recipes here. These are the jars with threaded necks and self-sealing lids. They are made of heavy enough glass to be safe when packed with hot food. Even so, each jar should be checked carefully and any with cracks or chips discarded.

The jars and lids should be washed in hot, soapy water, then rinsed with scalding water. Place them in a large, deep pan; cover them completely with hot water; and bring to a bubbling boil, maintaining that for 5 minutes. Then turn off the heat and let the pan stand while you complete the recipe. If the jars cool off before the food is ready, just reheat them. It is very important that all the jars be hot when filled with the hot food.

To remove a sterile jar from the pan, take a pair of tongs and grasp each jar just below its threaded neck, placing the jar right side up on a level surface (but never on a metal surface; the jar could crack). Pack the food one jar at a time, sealing each jar before the next is removed from the pan. Follow the manufacturer's directions for using the self-sealing lids. Should any jars fail to seal, either reheat the food and repack it, or be sure to use it promptly.

Opposite is but a small selection of store-bought pickles:

1. half-sour pickle
2. sour dill pickle
3. pickled onions
4. gherkins
5. pickled artichoke heart
6. picked yellow and red peppers
7. pickled cantaloupe
8. pickled green pepper
9. mixed pickles
10. cornichon
11. pickled green beans
12. pickled watermelon rind
13. capers
14. pickled baby corn on the cob
15. pickled button mushrooms
16. pickled carrots
17. pickled okra and red pepper
18. pickled cherries
19. pickled cherry pepper
20. pickled sour tomato

Mustard Pickles

(2 quarts)

2 cups ¼-inch-thick cucumber slices
1 cup green tomato wedges
1 cup diced red pepper
1 cup 1-inch-long string bean pieces
1 cup tiny white onions
1 cup 1-inch-long carrot strips
½ cup noniodized salt
1½ cups sugar
2 tablespoons dry mustard
2 teaspoons turmeric
1 tablespoon pickling spices
6 tablespoons all-purpose flour
2 cups cider vinegar

Combine the vegetables and salt in a 2- to 3-quart casserole and cover with water. Set aside to soak overnight.

Bring the vegetables to a boil, drain them thoroughly, and return them to the casserole.

Combine the sugar, mustard, turmeric, pickling spices, and flour in a 1- to 2-quart enamel or stainless steel saucepan. Gradually stir in the vinegar until the mixture is smooth and all the ingredients are well combined. Cook uncovered over moderate heat until the sauce thickens enough to coat a spoon heavily. Pour the sauce over the vegetables in the casserole, bring to a boil over high heat, then reduce the heat to moderate and simmer for 15 minutes.

Pack the pickles into hot, sterilized jars, seal tightly, and refrigerate.

Bread & Butter Pickles

(5 cups)

6 cups ¼-inch-thick cucumber slices
2 cups thinly sliced onions
¼ cup noniodized salt
¾ cup cider vinegar
¾ cup sugar
¼ teaspoon turmeric
1 tablespoon mustard seed
½ teaspoon celery seed
⅛ teaspoon cayenne

Combine the cucumbers and onions in a large bowl and stir in the salt. Set aside for 3 hours, then pour off any accumulated liquid. Rinse the vegetables in cold water and drain thoroughly.

Combine the vinegar, sugar, turmeric, mustard seed, celery seed, and cayenne in a 2- to 3-quart enamel or stainless steel casserole. Bring to a boil, stirring to be sure the ingredients are well combined. Add the cucumbers and onions. Bring back to a boil, then immediately pack into hot, sterilized jars, seal tightly, and refrigerate.

Mimi Sheraton's Garlic Dill Pickles

(24 - 30 pickles)

24-30	very firm, small kerby cucumbers, free of bruises or brown spots
7-8	cloves garlic, unpeeled but lightly crushed
1	teaspooon coriander seed
1	teaspooon mustard seed
1	teaspoon black peppercorns
4-5	small, dried hot red peppers, or ½ teaspoon crushed, dried hot red Italian peppers
3	bay leaves
12-14	sprigs fresh dill, preferably with seed heads, well washed
1	teaspoon dried dill seed heads, well washed (if dill has no seed heads, add 1 teaspoon dried dill seed)
¾	cup coarse salt
3	quarts of water, approximately

Wash a wide-mouthed bean pot, crock, or glass jar thoroughly. Wash the cucumbers and trim off any bruises.

Stand the cucumbers on end around sides and across the bottom of the crock or jar, so that they are held in place, but not so tightly packed that they crush one another. A second layer can be added if the jar is tall enough.

Add the garlic and all herbs and spices, including the dill sprigs, to the crock.

Add the salt to the water and stir until dissolved. Pour the salt water into the crock to completely cover the cucumbers. Brine should overflow so you can be sure no air pockets remain. If it does not, place the crock under the faucet and let water run in slowly until it does overflow.

Place jar on a stain-proof surface in a cool place—the temperature should be between 65° and 70°. Place a dish or wooden disk directly over pickles, in the brine, and weight it down with a clean stone or glass partially filled with water. Cover the crock loosely with a dish towel or a double thickness of cheesecloth.

Every 24 hours check the pickles and remove any white or gray foam that has risen to the surface. This will prevent rotting. Shake crock slightly to distribute the spices and be sure to replace the weight. If brine seems bland, add seasonings. Pickles will be half-pickled in about 5 days and completely pickled in about 10 days. Store in the refrigerator in tightly closed jars. Pour some strained brine into the jar to cover pickles.

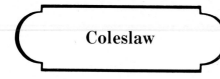

Coleslaw

(1½ pints)

3 tablespoons sugar
¼ cup cider vinegar
3 tablespoons vegetable oil
1 teaspoon dry mustard
1 teaspoon celery seed
1 teaspoon salt
Freshly ground black pepper
4 cups shredded cabbage
½ green pepper, cut into thin strips (½ cup)
½ cup grated carrots

Combine the sugar, vinegar, vegetable oil, mustard, celery seed, salt, and several grindings of black pepper in a 1-quart enamel or stainless steel saucepan. Bring to boil over a high heat.

Toss together, in a large bowl, the cabbage, onion, green pepper, and carrot. Pour the hot dressing over the raw vegetables and cool to room temperature. Refrigerate, tightly covered with plastic wrap or foil, for 24 hours before serving.

Corn Relish

(1 quart)

½ cup water
½ cup distilled white vinegar
¼ cup sugar
1 tablespoon noniodized salt
1 teaspoon turmeric
1 teaspoon celery seed
2 teaspoons dry mustard
1 cup finely chopped red pepper
1 cup finely chopped celery
½ cup finely chopped onion
2 10-ounce packages frozen corn kernels, or 4 cups fresh corn, cut from the cob

Combine the water, vinegar, sugar, salt, turmeric, celery seed, and mustard in a 2- to 3-quart enamel pot or stainless steel casserole. Stirring frequently with a wooden spoon, bring the mixture to a boil. Add the red pepper, celery, onion, and corn and return to a boil. Cook uncovered for 5 minutes, then pack the relish into hot, sterilized jars, seal tightly, and refrigerate.

Relishes: pepper-onion, coleslaw, Mexican salsa fria, corn

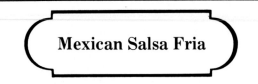

Mexican Salsa Fria

(1 pint)

- 2 pounds tomatoes, peeled, seeded, juiced, and chopped
- 1 teaspoon crushed red pepper
- 1 teaspoon salt
- 1 teaspoon pepper
- 1 large onion, chopped (½ cup)
- 1 clove garlic, crushed
- 2 tablespoons fresh lemon juice
- 1 tablespoon olive oil
- 1 Italian green pepper, chopped (½ cup)

Mix all the ingredients together in a large bowl. Chill for several hours, then drain in a colander before serving.

Combine the onion and pepper in a large bowl and cover them with boiling water. Let them sit for 5 minutes, then drain and repeat.

Place the mixture in a 2- to 2½-quart enamel pot or stainless steel casserole and stir in the sugar, vinegar, and salt. Bring to a boil and cook uncovered for 30 to 45 minutes, or until the mixture thickens. Pack the boiling hot relish into hot, sterilized jars, seal tightly, and refrigerate.

Pepper-Onion Relish

(1 quart)

- 1 large onion, finely chopped (2 cups)
- 1 medium red pepper, finely chopped (1 cup)
- ¼ cup sugar
- 1 cup cider vinegar
- 1 teaspoon noniodized salt

TWO
The Sandwiches

Tea & Cocktail Sandwiches

Savory little sandwiches, salty nuts, sweet cakes, and cookies are traditional tea time fare. The tea should be piping hot—if it's hot tea that's being served; during summer, iced tea might be preferable.

To brew a proper pot of hot tea, fill a kettle with cold water and bring the water to a boil. Pour a small amount of boiling water into the teapot to warm it. Empty the water out of the teapot and add tea, a teaspoon of loose tea for each cup to be served plus one for the pot. When the water in the kettle reaches a rolling boil, pour it into the pot. Allow the tea to steep for 3 to 5 minutes before serving.

For iced tea, pour hot tea over cracked ice or ice cubes in individual glasses or in a pitcher. Since the tea will be diluted by the melting ice, let it steep until strong before pouring it over ice. A metal spoon inside each glass or the pitcher will dissipate the heat from the tea enough to prevent cracking.

Besides tea, it is nice to provide other sorts of drinks: coffee and hot chocolate during the cold months; during the warm months, iced coffee, fruit juice, and soft drinks.

Cocktails call for sandwiches that are on the more substantial side, and lots of them. Also lots of nuts, pickles, olives (best at room temperature), and raw vegetables. And plenty of good drink. And tons of ice.

If you don't have a fully equipped bar, it's probably best to stick to just two types of mixed cocktails. But be sure to offer wine, soft drinks, and mineral water: more and more people prefer these lighter drinks.

If you want to have all the basic liquors on hand, you'll need at least 1 kind of gin, 2 kinds of vermouth (sweet and dry), 4 kinds of whiskey (blended whiskey, bourbon, Scotch and Canadian), and vodka—and maybe a bottle of rum. You'll also need the basic mixers: club soda, tonic water, quinine water, Bitter Lemon, ginger ale, 7-Up. And depending on how complete you want to be, you may want these accessories: bitters, Worcestershire sauce, cherries, cocktail onions, olives, lemons, limes, Rose's lime juice, and orange, tomato, and vegetable juices.

Tea sandwiches: cream cheese and salami, cucumber rounds

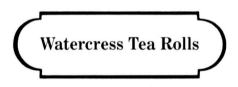

Blue Cheese & Apple Slices

(8 cocktail sandwiches)

1 red Delicious apple, unpeeled, cored, and thinly sliced
Blue Cheese Butter, softened
4 slices whole wheat bread, with crusts removed

Spread all 4 slices of the bread with a good layer of blue cheese butter. Arrange slices of apple over 2 of the bread slices and top with the remaining bread. Cut the sandwiches into fourths.

Watercress Tea Rolls

(4 tea sandwiches)

½ bunch watercress
4 very thin slices white bread, with crusts removed
2 tablespoons butter, *or* cream cheese, softened

Wash the watercress in cold water, pat dry, and remove and discard the main stems.

Flatten the bread with a rolling pin or a bottle, then spread generously with butter or cream cheese. Place several sprigs of water-cress at one end of each slice of bread and roll the bread up around the watercress. For prettier-looking rolls, make sure some leaves stick out a tiny bit over either side of the bread, so they show when the bread is rolled. To keep the sandwiches firmly rolled, wrap them in a damp towel or plastic wrap and chill before serving.

Sour Cream & Caviar Sandwiches

(4 open-face sandwiches)

4 slices seedless rye or pumpernickel bread
1 2-ounce jar red, black, or lumpfish caviar
½ cup sour cream
1 hard-boiled egg, chopped fine
Paprika

Toast the bread on one side. Gently mix the caviar and the sour cream together, and spread on the untoasted side of the bread. Garnish with a sprinkling of chopped egg and paprika.

Salmony Cucumber Sandwiches

(16 cocktail sandwiches)

1   cucumber
8   very thin slices pumpernickel
    bread, with crusts removed
½   cup Smoked Salmon Butter
    softened

If the cucumber is heavily waxed, peel it or score it lengthwise with the tines of a fork, then cut into thin slices. Place the slices in a colander and salt generously, leaving them for at least ½ hour. This will remove excess water. Dry the slices on paper towels.

Spread all 8 slices of pumpernickel bread with the salmon butter. Cover 4 slices of the buttered bread with cucumber slices, and top with the remaining 4 slices of bread. Cut into triangles, squares, or oblongs.

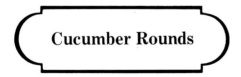

Cucumber Rounds

(3 dozen open-face sandwiches)

1   cucumber
9   very thin slices white bread, with
    crusts removed
¼   cup Onion Mayonnaise
Finely chopped fresh dill

If the cucumber is heavily waxed, peel it or score it lengthwise with the tines of a fork. Then, with a vegetable peeler or sharp knife, slice the cucumber paper thin.

Use a plain round cookie or biscuit cutter to cut 4 circles out of each slice of bread. Spread the rounds with Onion mayonnaise, top with 2 or 3 cucumber slices and garnish with a sprinkling of dill.

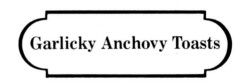

Garlicky Anchovy Toasts

(16 cocktail squares)

4   ounces cream cheese, softened
3   tablespoons anchovy paste
1½   tablespoons grated onion
½   tablespoon chopped fresh chives
1   teaspoon fresh lemon juice
1   teaspoon Worcestershire sauce
3   cloves garlic, crushed
Yogurt
4   slices white bread, toasted, with
     crusts removed, cut into fourths

Mix the cream cheese with the anchovy paste, onion, chives, lemon juice, Worcestershire sauce, and garlic. Blend well. If the mixture seems too thick to spread, lighten it by adding yogurt, a spoonful at a time, until the desired consistency is reached. Spread on the toasted squares.

Anchovy & Pimiento Sandwiches

(16 cocktail sandwiches)

8 slices white bread
½ cup Anchovy Butter, softened
1 4-ounce jar whole pimientos
Freshly ground black pepper

Spread all 8 slices with anchovy butter and cover 4 of the buttered slices with layers of pimiento. Grind black pepper over the pimiento and top with the remaining bread. Cut each sandwich into fourths.

Cream Cheese & Salami Spectaculars

(8 open-face sandwiches)

4 ounces cream cheese, softened
1 tablespoon horseradish
8 very thin slices salami
2 very thin slices white bread, cut into fourths

Blend the cream cheese with the horseradish and spread lavishly on the salami. Roll the salami slices into cone shapes and place each on a square of bread.

Deli Numbers

(12 open-face sandwiches)

Three simple sandwiches that serve as more substantial cocktail fare:

12 slices pumpernickel or rye bread
Mayonnaise
4 slices roast beef
¼ cup Russian Dressing
4 slices tongue
¼ cup pickle relish
4 slices turkey breast
¼ cup Green Mayonnaise

Spread all 12 slices of bread lightly with mayonnaise.

Spread roast beef with Russian dressing, tongue with pickle relish, and turkey with green mayonnaise. Fold each in half and place on bread. Or arrange a platter of the cold meats and set out with a basket of bread and bowls of mayonnaise, relish, and dressing for guests to assemble their own sandwiches.

Open-face deli sandwiches: roast beef with Russian dressing, cream cheese and salami, tongue with pickle relish, turkey with green mayonnaise

Homemade Country Pâté

(4 pounds pâté)

2 slices white bread
4 tablespoons milk
1⅓ pounds pork or chicken livers
1⅓ pounds lean ground pork
1⅓ pounds ground pork fat
1 egg, lightly beaten
3 bay leaves, crushed fine
¾ teaspoon dried thyme
1½ tablespoons freshly ground black pepper
¼ cup vermouth
¼ cup cognac
⅓ cup finely chopped onion
1 clove garlic, crushed, or 2 shallots, finely chopped
3 sprigs parsley, finely chopped
½ pound bacon, blanched

Preheat the oven to 300°. Crumble the bread into the milk and set aside.

Liquefy the liver in a food processor or blender, then mix it with the ground pork and pork fat in a large bowl. Mix in the rest of the ingredients and the soaked bread and blend well. To test for flavor, sauté a spoonful of the mixture in a small skillet and taste it. If necessary, add more seasonings. The paté should be highly seasoned.

Line a 1½-quart loaf pan with strips of blanched bacon. Arrange the strips length-wise or crosswise, making sure they cover the bottom and sides of the pan. Keep aside enough strips to cover the top.

Spoon the meat mixture into the bacon-lined loaf pan, smoothing with a spoon or spatula and arranging strips of blanched bacon over the top. Cover the loaf pan securely with aluminum foil, crimping the edges to seal tightly. Poke a small hole in the center of the foil so the steam can escape.

Place the loaf pan in a larger pan and pour enough cold water in the larger pan to reach halfway up the side of the loaf pan. Bake for 3 hours. Remove from the oven, allow to cool, then refrigerate overnight.

Guy Pascal's Pâté Sandwiches

(8 open-face sandwiches)

4 croissants
8 slices *pâté de campagne* (country-style meat pâté), *or* imported salami
6-8 cornichons (imported tiny gherkins)

Using a serrated knife, split each croissant in half to form two crescent shapes. Cut each slice of pâté to fit the crescent shape and lightly press the pâté into the roll with a spreading knife. Cut the cornichons lengthwise into very thin slices and arrange in a leaf pattern over the pâté.

Cheddar & Port Wine Squares

(16 cocktail sandwiches)

> 5 ounces sharp Cheddar cheese, finely grated
> 1 ounce cream cheese, softened
> 2 tablespoons port wine
> 4 very thin slices pumpernickel bread, cut into fourths

Combine the grated Cheddar with the cream cheese and port wine. Blend until smooth. (A food processor does an excellent job of this, but you can also mix by hand, or use an electric mixer or blender.) Spread generously on the pumpernickel squares.

Brie & Vermouth Squares

(16 cocktail sandwiches)

> 3 ounces Brie, rind removed
> 1 ounce cream cheese, softened
> 2 tablespoons dry vermouth
> 1 teaspoon finely chopped parsley
> 4 very thin slices dark pumpernickel bread, cut into fourths

Blend together the Brie, cream cheese, dry vermouth, and parsley—by hand, or in an electric mixer, blender, or food processor. Refrigerate overnight to enhance the flavor. Serve at room temperature on pumpernickel squares.

Herb & Cream Cheese Squares

(16 cocktail sandwiches)

> 4 ounces cream cheese, softened
> 2 tablespoons finely chopped fresh dill; or 1 tablespoon each finely chopped fresh basil and fresh chives; or 1 tablespoon each finely chopped fresh chervil and fresh chives
> 1½ tablespoons finely chopped parsley
> ¼ teaspoon freshly ground black pepper
> Worcestershire sauce
> 4 very thin slices rye bread, cut into fourths

Combine the cream cheese with the dill, parsley, and black pepper. Add Worcestershire sauce to taste. Refrigerate the mixture for at least 12 hours to enhance the flavor. Serve at room temperature on rye squares.

Lunchtime Favorites

Whether you eat at home, pack a lunch box, or brown bag it, lunchtime usually means a sandwich, maybe a piece of fruit or nuts and raisins, a couple of cookies or bag of potato chips. Potato chips in a sandwich add a wonderfully salty, crunchy touch, especially if the sandwich is of plain bologna or luncheon meat. (But then everyone has his favorite concoctions.)

Lunchtime sandwiches usually fall into several specific categories. One of these is egg salad, which calls for hard-boiled eggs. For those of you who lament that you can't boil an egg, here is a reliable method (these instructions are for large eggs): Put the eggs in a pot of cold water. It is best if the eggs are at room temperature. Add a teaspoon of salt and a few drops of vinegar. (In case of any cracks, the vinegar in the water helps the egg white to coagulate and keeps it from oozing out.) Bring the water to a boil, then reduce the heat and simmer the eggs for no more than 12 minutes. Do not boil them or you will get a dark line around the yolk. Immediately empty the hot water from the pot and cool the eggs under very cold water. This will shrink the egg from the shell and make peeling easier.

Grilled cheese is one of the all-time favorite sandwiches. Here is a unique technique for grilling that deserves mention: Grilled Cheese à la Mary Alice (she's someone who doesn't like to cook, and hardly ever turns on the stove; she's been doing cheese sandwiches this way for years). For each sandwich put the desired amount of cheese between two pieces of white bread. Butter the outside of the bread on both sides of the sandwich and wrap the sandwich in foil this way: Place the sandwich in the middle of a piece of foil, fold one side of the foil over so that it completely covers the top of the sandwich, then fold over the other side. Do not roll the foil closed or crimp it together in the middle–you will get an untoasted band of sandwich that way. Fold the foil in a bit on the sides. Now plug in an iron (!) and put it on the highest setting. When it is hot, place the iron on the sandwich for 20 seconds. Turn the sandwich over and iron for another 20 seconds. It works perfectly and tastes terrific! It's fast, it's neat, and it's safe. Just be sure to turn the iron off when the sandwich is done.

Peanut butter and jelly sandwich

The Purist's Peanut Butter

(½ cup)

1 6¼-ounce can salted peanuts

Place the nuts in a peanut butter machine, a blender, or a food processor and purée into a smooth butter. If dry roasted nuts are used, the peanut butter may be too dry: add up to 1 tablespoon vegetable oil. If unsalted peanuts (available at health food stores) are used, add salt to taste.

HONEY PEANUT BUTTER: Blend in 2 tablespoons of honey.

OTHER NUT BUTTERS: Cashew butter, pecan butter, and walnut butter are made in exactly the same way as Peanut Butter—by puréeing.

Cream Cheese & Olive Sandwiches

(4 sandwiches)

4 ounces cream cheese, softened
¼ cup Mayonnaise
½ cup chopped pimiento-stuffed green olives
8 very thin slices white bread, with crusts removed

Combine the cream cheese with the mayonnaise and blend well. Mix in the olives. Spread on 4 slices of bread. Top with the remaining slices.

BLACK OLIVE VARIATION: For the green olives, substitute ½ cup chopped black olives and add 1 teaspoon Dijon mustard.

Chopped Chicken Liver Sandwiches

(4 sandwiches)

4 tablespoons butter
1 clove garlic, crushed
1 pound chicken livers
½ teaspoon salt
Freshly ground black pepper
8 slices rye bread
Lettuce and tomato (optional)

Melt the butter with the garlic in a skillet over moderately high heat. Sauté the chicken livers 5 to 7 minutes, or until there is no trace of pink inside. Remove the livers to a wide bowl and chop fine. Season to taste with salt and pepper. Spread on rye bread, add lettuce and tomato, and top with remaining bread.

WITH BACON: Crumble 2 slices of cooked bacon into the above recipe and mix. Serve on white toast.

WITH RAW ONIONS: Add 2 teaspoons finely chopped onion, 1 tablespoon chopped parsley, and cayenne to taste. Serve on pumpernickel bread.

WITH SAUTÉED CHOPPED ONIONS: Sauté ¼ cup chopped onions in butter until lightly browned. Mix into the chopped liver along with 1 teaspoon chopped fresh tarragon.

WITH EGG: Chop 1 hard-boiled egg and blend into the chopped liver. Serve on white bread with lettuce.

Spicy Corned Beef Sandwiches

(4 sandwiches)

1 cup finely chopped corned beef
2 tablespoons grated onion
1 tablespoon horseradish
1 teaspoon Dijon mustard
2 tablespoons mayonnaise
8 slices sour rye or Swedish rye bread

Combine the corned beef with the onion, horseradish, and mustard. Add the 2 tablespoons of mayonnaise, or more if desired. Spread on 4 slices of rye bread, top with the remaining bread.

Meatloaf Sandwiches

(4 sandwiches)

8 slices meatloaf (*see* recipe below)
Honeyed Ketchup
8 slices white or rye bread
Butter

Butter the bread. Arrange 2 slices of meatloaf on each of 4 slices of bread. Spread with ketchup and top with the remaining bread.

Meatloaf:
1 pound ground beef
½ pound ground veal
½ pound ground pork
¾ cup packaged herb stuffing mix
2 tablespoons dried onion soup mix
2 large eggs
1 cup milk
Freshly ground black pepper

Preheat the oven to 350°. Oil a round or square pie or cake pan.

Place all the ingredients in a large bowl and mix thoroughly, using your hands or a wooden spoon. Pile the meat mixture into the middle of the oiled pan and pat into a round or oblong shape. Bake for 1¼ hours. The meatloaf will keep in the refrigerator for at least a week.

Meaty Combinations

(Sandwich-meat-and ... suggestions, some may be old favorites, some may become new ones.)

Bologna and cream cheese
Bologna and Monterey Jack cheese
Bologna and Swiss cheese
Corned beef and coleslaw
Corned beef and sliced dill pickle
Corned beef, Swiss cheese, and onion
Corned beef, Swiss cheese, and tomato
Ham and Cheddar cheese
Ham, cream cheese, and mustard
Ham, cream cheese, and pineapple
Ham, cream cheese, and scallions
Ham and Swiss cheese
Ham, Swiss cheese, and sauerkraut
Liverwurst and bacon
Liverwurst, bacon, and tomato
Liverwurst, cucumber, and tomato
Liverwurst and Swiss cheese
Liverwurst and sliced egg
Pastrami, tomato, and Cheddar cheese
Pepperoni, provolone, and tomato
Salami and sliced egg
Roast beef, Cheddar cheese, tomato, and
   Russian Dressing
Roast beef, Swiss cheese, and bacon
Turkey, ham, asparagus, and tomato
Turkey, bacon, and tomato
Turkey, ham, and Swiss cheese

Chicken Salad Sandwiches

(4 sandwiches)

1 cup diced cooked chicken
3 tablespoons chopped celery
¼ cup Mayonnaise
Salt and freshly ground black pepper
8 slices white or whole wheat bread
Mayonnaise
4 lettuce leaves

In a bowl mix the chicken with the celery and mayonnaise. Add salt and pepper to taste.

Spread all 8 slices of bread with mayonnaise. Spread chicken salad on 4 slices. Top each sandwich with a lettuce leaf and another slice of bread.

WITH WALNUTS: Add ¼ cup coarsely chopped walnuts. For apples and walnuts, use only 2 tablespoons coarsely chopped walnuts and add 2 tablespoons coarsely chopped apple.

WITH ALMONDS & WATER CHESTNUTS: Add ¼ cup chopped almonds, and substitute water chestnuts for the celery.

(Preceding pages) A selection of deli meats

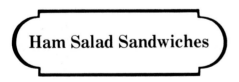

Milton Glaser's Chicken Salad Sandwiches

(2 sandwiches)

1 cup diced cooked chicken
2 tablespoons Mayonnaise
2 teaspoons soy sauce
¼ cup sliced scallions
2 tablespoons toasted sesame seed
Salt and freshly ground black pepper
Fresh coriander
8 slices white or whole wheat bread

In a bowl mix the chicken with the mayonnaise and soy sauce. Blend in the scallions and sesame seed. Season with salt and pepper and garnish with fresh coriander.

Spread 4 slices of bread with chicken salad. Top with the remaining bread.

Ham Salad Sandwiches

(4 sandwiches)

1 cup chopped cooked ham
3 tablespoons chopped celery
1 tablespoon minced parsley
3 tablespoons Mayonnaise
1 tablespoon Dijon mustard
8 slices rye bread

Put the ham with the celery, parsley, mayonnaise, and mustard in a bowl. Mix until well blended.

Spread 4 slices of bread with ham salad. Top with the remaining bread.

Shrimp & Artichoke Salad Sandwiches

(4 sandwiches)

1 cup chopped cooked shrimp
½ cup chopped artichoke bottoms
2 tablespoons fresh lemon juice
¼ cup Mayonnaise
1 tablespoon horseradish
Salt and freshly ground black pepper
8 slices white bread

Combine the shrimp, artichoke bottoms, lemon juice, mayonnaise, and horseradish, mixing until well blended. Add salt and pepper to taste.

Spread 4 slices of bread with shrimp and artichoke salad. Top with the remaining bread.

Tuna Salad Sandwiches

(6 sandwiches)

2 6 ½-ounce cans chunk white tuna, drained
½ cup Mayonnaise
Juice of 1 lemon
Freshly ground black pepper
12 slices white, whole wheat, or rye bread

Empty the cans of tuna into a medium-sized bowl. Stir in the mayonnaise, squeeze in the lemon juice, and add black pepper to taste. Mix until well blended.

Spread 6 slices of bread with tuna salad. Top with the remaining bread.

CRUNCHY TUNA SALAD: Add ¼ cup of each of the following ingredients, chopped: celery, tart apple, cucumber, and red onion.

REAL HOT TUNA SALAD: Substitute the juice of 1 lime for the lemon juice in the master recipe and add 1 heaping tablespoon of horseradish.

TUNA SALAD FINES HERBES: Add ¼ cup chopped fresh herbs, using a mix of at least two of the following: basil, chives, dill, oregano, parsley, rosemary, savory, tarragon. Add white pepper to taste. (This is delicious on toasted cheese bread.)

Egg Salad Sandwiches

(6-8 sandwiches)

8 hard-boiled eggs
½ cup Mayonnaise
Juice of ½ lemon
½ teaspoon dry mustard
¼ teaspoon salt
¼ teaspoon white pepper
12-16 slices rye, pumpernickel, or toasted white bread

Peel the hard-boiled eggs and put them in a medium-sized bowl. Chop them fine with a chopper or knife, or break them up with the side of a fork. Add the mayonnaise and stir until blended. Then squeeze half a lemon into the mixture and add the mustard, salt, and white pepper. Stir until well blended.

Spread 6 to 8 slices of bread with egg salad. Top with remaining bread.

DILLED EGG SALAD: Add 4 teaspoons Dijon mustard and 4 teaspoons chopped fresh dill.

INDIAN EGG SALAD: Add 2 ½ tablespoons chopped preserved ginger and 2 teaspoons hot Madras curry powder. (You might try this variation on Apple Walnut Bread.)

OLIVE & EGG SALAD: Add ½ cup chopped green or black olives to the master recipe.

Tuna salad sandwich

Sardine Bagelwiches

(2 sandwiches)

1 can boneless sardines, packed in olive oil
2 bagels
1 3-ounce package cream cheese, softened
1 small red onion, very thinly sliced
1 tomato, sliced
Lettuce

Drain the sardines and mash them in a bowl.

Split the bagels and spread all four halves with cream cheese. Spread mashed sardines onto two of the bagel halves, add slices of onion, slices of tomato, lettuce, and top with the remaining 2 bagel halves.

Sprouts Salad Sandwiches

(2 sandwiches)

Anchovy Butter
4 slices cracked wheat bread, *or* 2 pitas
4 tablespoons alfalfa sprouts
1 large mushroom, thinly sliced
10 cherry tomatoes, cut in half, or 1 medium tomato, sliced

Spread anchovy butter on all 4 slices of bread. Sprinkle 2 slices with sprouts, and then arrange layers of mushroom slices and cherry tomato halves to cover. Top with the remaining bread.

VARIATION: Substitute sweet butter for the anchovy butter and add a generous layer (about 2 tablespoons) of crumbled Gorgonzola cheese.

Spinach Salad Sandwiches

(4 sandwiches)

1 pound fresh spinach
1 avocado
8 slices rye or pumpernickel bread, *or* 4 pitas
10 slices cooked bacon
2 hard-boiled eggs, sliced
2 mushrooms, thinly sliced
1 red onion, very thinly sliced
Mayonnaise

Wash the spinach, remove the stems, and dry the leaves on paper towels.

Mash the avocado, spread onto 4 slices of bread, and sprinkle liberally with salt. Crumble the bacon onto the avocado. Arrange egg, mushroom slices, and onion slices over the bacon, and then add spinach leaves. Spread mayonnaise on the 4 remaining slices of bread, and place on top of the spinach layer.

Carrot & Apple Sandwiches

(2 sandwiches)

4 slices health bread
Almond Butter
1 red Delicious apple, peeled, cored, and thinly sliced
1 small carrot, sliced into thin rounds

Spread all 4 slices of health bread with a lavish amount of almond butter. Arrange an apple and carrot layer on 2 of the 4 slices of bread, alternating a single apple slice with several carrot rounds. Top with the remaining bread.

Grilled Cheddar & Tomato Sandwiches

(4 sandwiches)

Butter
8 slices white bread
4 slices Cheddar cheese
1 large tomato, sliced
Salt and freshly ground black pepper
¼ cup butter or margarine, melted

Lightly butter the bread and top each of 4 slices with a slice of Cheddar. Add tomato slices and salt and pepper. Top with the remaining bread. To grill, brush both sides of the sandwich with melted butter, place in a skillet or under the broiler, and cook for 5 minutes on each side, or until the bread is browned and the cheese bubbling. (This sandwich is also good without grilling.)

WITH BACON: Cook 8 slices of bacon until crispy and place 2 slices on each sandwich, between the cheese and the tomato.

Grilled Swiss & Zucchini Sandwiches

(4 sandwiches)

4 slices white bread, toasted
Garlic Butter
1 medium onion, very thinly sliced
1 medium zucchini, very thinly sliced
4 slices Swiss cheese
Grated Parmesan cheese

Preheat the broiler.
Spread the toast with garlic butter. To each of the 4 slices, add slices of onion, slices of zucchini, a slice of Swiss, and a heavy sprinkling of Parmesan. Broil 3 to 5 minutes, or until the cheese melts.

The All-American Hot Dog & Hamburger

Hot dogs and hamburgers are popular just about everywhere today. The versions that caught on in America around the turn of this century originated in Germany (in Frankfurt and Hamburg), but the practice of extending meat by grinding or chopping and then seasoning it before cooking is age-old, as is the practice of stuffing such mixtures into casings for convenience in storing and cooking and for longer life. "Sausages," of which hot dogs are a derivative, have a long history in many European cuisines, and recipes for dishes using ground meat patties abound in Middle Eastern and Oriental cooking as well.

The simplest way to cook hot dogs is to put them in a large pot of water and bring the water to a boil. At that point, cover the pan, lower the heat, and simmer for 5 minutes. To pan-broil them, melt a tiny bit of butter in a large skillet, add the hot dogs, and heat until browned.

Some aficionados will tell you the best frankfurters are grilled—whole or split—in an oven broiler or over a charcoal fire. This method makes a hot dog that's juicy and tender inside, and crisp on the outside, for a satisfying crunch when you bite into it.

The healthiest way to cook a hamburger is oven broiling. It is also the easiest. Preheat the broiler and place the patties 4 inches from the heat. A 1"-thick patty will be "rare" after 3 minutes in the broiler on each side.

There are two ways to pan-broil, or sauté, hamburgers—with or without added fat or oil. Cooks usually have strong opinions about the merits of one over the other. Either method will produce juicy flavorful hamburgers if done properly, but cooking without added fat is probably better for you.

Preheat an ungreased heavy skillet. When it is hot enough for the meat to sizzle, add the patties and cook them over moderately high heat for 3 minutes, then turn them with a spatula. (Enough fat should have been released from the meat so the patties will not stick.) A popular variation calls for scattering salt over the surface of the preheated pan. But if too much salt is added, it will draw the juices out of the meat into the pan. The patties will not stick, but they may not be as juicy as they would be otherwise.

To pan-broil hamburgers in an oiled skillet, melt 1 tablespoon of butter and 1 tablespoon of oil in a skillet. When the pan is hot, sear the meat quickly on both sides over high heat (to seal in the juices). Reduce heat and cook to desired doneness, turning once more in the process.

Some people will tell you the best hamburgers are barbecued—broiled over an open charcoal fire (probably the same people who like their hot dogs done this way). Barbecuing does impart a wonderfully smoky flavor to the meat that no other method of cooking— and no seasoning—can match.

Hot dog with mustard and sauerkraut

Hot Dog Sandwiches with Apples & Onions

(4 sandwiches)

2-4 tablespoons butter
4 frankfurters, slit almost all the way through at quarter-inch intervals along their length
1 large onion, thinly sliced
1 large red Delicious apple, peeled, cored, and thickly sliced
4 hamburger rolls, *or* 8 slices rye bread

Melt 2 tablespoons of butter in a large skillet over moderately high heat. When the butter is foaming, add the frankfurters and fry 5 to 10 minutes, or until they start to curl. Remove the franks from the skillet and drain on paper towels.

Add the onion slices to the skillet and cook until they are soft and translucent, about 5 minutes. Then add the apple slices and, if necessary, more butter. Cover the pan, lower the heat, and cook for about 5 minutes, or until the apple slices can be pierced easily with a fork. Return the frankfurters to the pan, cover, and cook until they are heated through. The franks will be circular in shape.

Open 4 hamburger rolls, place 1 frankfurter in each, and spoon on the apples and onions.

Hot Chihuahuas

(12-16 sandwiches)

Chili Con Carne:
2 tablespoons butter
½ cup chopped onion
1 clove garlic, crushed
1 pound ground beef
1 1-pound can tomatoes
1 20-ounce can kidney beans
1 bay leaf
1 teaspoon salt
2 teaspoons chili powder
12-16 hot dogs
12-16 hot dog rolls

Melt the butter in a skillet over moderately high heat. Add the onion and garlic and sauté until the onion is soft. Add the meat, breaking it up with a fork, and fry slowly until the meat is no longer pink. Stir in the other ingredients, cover, and simmer for at least 1 hour. Remove the bay leaf before serving.

Grill, broil, or boil the hot dogs, as desired, and place one in each roll. Spoon the chili over each and serve.

Hot Dogs with Baked Beans

(4 sandwiches)

> 1 small can pea beans with brown sugar
> 1 tablespoon brown sugar
> 2 tablespoons ketchup
> 1 tablespoon prepared mustard
> 4 hot dogs
> 4 hot dog rolls

In a saucepan mix the pea beans with the brown sugar, ketchup, and mustard, and simmer over medium heat for 10 minutes.

Grill, broil, or boil the hot dogs, as desired, and place one in each roll. Spoon the beans over each and serve.

Sausage & Pepper Dogs

(8 sandwiches)

> 1 large onion, sliced
> 3 tablespoons olive oil
> 2 green peppers, cut into strips
> 2 sweet red peppers, cut into strips
> 1 clove garlic, crushed
> Salt and freshly ground black pepper
> 8 sweet Italian sausages
> 2 tablespoons water
> 8 hot dog rolls

Heat the oil in a large skillet, add the onion, and sauté until lightly browned. Add the peppers, along with the crushed garlic clove. Season with salt and pepper to taste. Cook, stirring occasionally, until the peppers are soft, about 20 to 25 minutes.

While the peppers and onions are cooking, start the sausages. Prick them so they won't burst, then place in a large skillet with 2 tablespoons of water, and cook over medium heat until brown, about 15 to 20 minutes.

Add a cooked sausage and a heaping layer of peppers and onions to each roll.

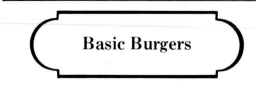

Basic Burgers

(4 sandwiches)

  1 pound lean ground beef (chuck or
     round)
  Salt and freshly ground black pepper
  1 tablespoon butter
  1 tablespoon oil
  4 hamburger rolls

Shape the meat into 4 patties. Be careful not to handle the meat too much. Too much handling toughens the meat by pressing out some of its moisture. Sprinkle with salt and pepper.

Melt the butter and oil in a skillet over moderately high heat and add the meat patties, searing on both sides. Reduce the heat to low and cook to desired doneness.

Serve on toasted or untoasted hamburger rolls, spread with butter, mayonnaise, mustard, ketchup, relish, or left plain.

HAWAIIAN BURGERS: Melt a little butter in a skillet and sauté slices of pineapple and slices of boiled ham until heated through. Place a slice of each on cooked burgers.

BORDEAUX BURGERS: Shape the Basic Burgers into patties, then sprinkle 1 tablespoon chopped parsley over each, and marinate in 1 cup of red wine for at least 2 hours before cooking.

BLUE CHEESE BURGERS: Cook the Basic Burgers and remove from pan, pouring off any fat that remains. Add 1 tablespoon of cream and 1 tablespoon of blue cheese to pan for each burger. Stir over low heat until the cheese melts, then pour over the burgers.

Favorite Hamburger Combinations

Cheeseburger (Swiss, Cheddar, and so on)
Bacon cheeseburger
Chiliburger
Pizza burger (with mozzarella cheese, a sprinkling of oregano and basil, and a spoonful of tomato sauce—good on English muffins)
Cheeseburger or bacon cheeseburger with fried onions and fried mushrooms
Colorado burger (that's with lettuce, tomato and mayonnaise)
Mexican burger (with onions and guacamole)

Cheeseburger with tomato, onion, and fried mushrooms

Burgers Lindström

(After a favorite Swedish recipe)

(4 sandwiches)

- 1 tablespoon butter
- 2 tablespoons finely chopped onion
- 1 pound lean ground beef
- 1 tablespoon capers, chopped
- 2 eggs
- ½ cup cream
- 3 tablespoons finely chopped pickled beets

Salt and freshly ground black pepper
- 3 tablespoons butter
- 2 tablespoons oil
- 4 hamburger rolls

Melt 1 tablespoon of butter in a skillet over moderately high heat and sauté the onion until it is soft but not brown. Mix the sautéed onion with the beef, capers, eggs, cream, and beets and shape into 4 patties. Sprinkle generously with salt and pepper.

Melt the butter and oil together in a large, heavy skillet and sauté the patties over moderately high heat until brown on both sides. Reduce the heat and cook to desired doneness. Serve in hamburger rolls.

Pork & Veal Burgers

(4 sandwiches)

- ½ pound ground veal
- ½ pound ground pork
- 1 medium onion, grated
- ½ cup bread crumbs
- ¼ cup cream
- 1 teaspoon chopped parsley

Salt
- ¼ teaspoon freshly ground black pepper
- 4 tablespoons butter
- 2 tablespoons vegetable oil
- 4 hamburger rolls, *or* 8 slices rye bread

Pickled beets (optional)

Mix the ground meats with the onion and the bread crumbs. Gradually beat in the cream until the mixture is light and fluffy. Add the parsley, salt and pepper and blend well. Refrigerate for 1 hour.

Shape into 4 patties. Place the butter and oil in a large skillet over high heat. When the butter has stopped foaming, lower the heat to moderate and add the patties. Cook about 10 minutes on each side, or until the meat is nicely browned and the juices show no tinge of pink.

Serve on hamburger rolls or rye bread and top with pickled beets.

Stella Standard's Lamb Burgers

(4 sandwiches)

1 pound lean ground lamb
1 medium onion, grated
1 teaspoon grated lime rind
1 teaspoon fresh lime juice
¼ teaspoon ground nutmeg
1 teaspoon ground cumin
Salt and freshly ground black pepper
1 egg
2 tablespoons dry sherry
Oil
4 hamburger rolls

Mix the lamb together with all the other ingredients and shape into 4 patties. Brush them with oil and broil or fry to a nice brown, about 6 minutes each side. Serve on hamburger rolls.

Corned Beef Hashburgers

(4 sandwiches)

1 15-ounce can corned beef hash
2 tablespoons butter
4 eggs
4 hamburger rolls

Shape the hash into 4 patties of equal size. Melt the butter in a hot skillet and add the hash patties. Cook, turning once, until they are brown and crispy on both sides.

While the hash is browning, poach the eggs and toast the rolls. Place a browned patty on each roll, top with a poached egg, and cover with the other half of the roll.

Heroics

Finishing one of these monumental sandwiches may seem a "heroic" task before the fact. But they're so good they'll be gone before you knew you could eat so much. Look at Dagwood. Perhaps you thought he was just emptying the refrigerator onto two pieces of bread, but the artistry was in his layering of the ingredients. No wonder he fought so hard against Alexander and Daisy and the pups to keep his creation all to himself.

Like Dagwood's sandwiches, all the recipes in this chapter call for combinations of foods that complement one another in taste and texture. That blending of elements is the secret of the enduring popularity of the Club Sandwich—standard fare, really, but somehow so much more satisfying than other, lesser combinations of the same ingredients. And it's the key to the incredible appeal of the more exotic Reuben sandwich, and our Ham & Crab Rolls.

Sandwiches such as the Poor Boy and Michael Batterberry's Greek Salad Hero are not only appetizing, but are wonderfully simple to prepare. Just split and spread the bread, layer the filling on the bottom half, cover with the top half, slice and serve. The elements are very basic—slices of meat, cheese, tomatoes, onion; the preparation, mere assembly.

Even the Fried Oyster Hero is very straightforward once you prepare the oysters for sautéing. Toast the bread while the oysters are cooking and then spread the loaf with sauce while the oysters are draining. In a very short amount of time, you'll have constructed a very impressive sandwich. Then you'll be the hero.

The Classic Club & Classy Variations

(4 sandwiches)

12 slices white bread
Mayonnaise
8   slices turkey breast
12 slices cooked bacon
2   tomatoes, sliced
Lettuce

Toast the bread, trim the crusts, and spread slices with mayonnaise. Use 3 slices for each sandwich. On the first slice of toast arrange two slices of turkey and cover with a second piece of toast. Top with 3 slices of bacon, tomato slices, and lettuce, and cover with the third piece of toast.

CLASSY VARIATION NO. 1

1   tablespoon Dijon mustard
¼   cup Mayonnaise
12 slices pumpernickel bread
8   slices smoked salmon
Dilled Egg Salad

Mix the mustard with the mayonnaise and spread on the bread. Stack the layers this way: a slice of bread topped with 2 slices of smoked salmon, topped with another slice of bread, topped with dilled egg salad, topped with the third slice of bread.

CLASSY VARIATION NO. 2

12 slices white bread
Mayonnaise
12 slices cooked bacon
2   tomatoes, sliced
Coleslaw, drained
8   slices Swiss cheese

Toast the bread and spread the slices with mayonnaise. On the first slice of bread place 3 strips of bacon and slices of tomato, top with a second slice of bread. Place a small heaping of coleslaw on this second slice of bread and top with 2 slices of Swiss cheese. Cover with the last slice of bread.

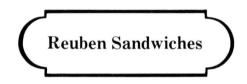

Reuben Sandwiches

(4 sandwiches)

1   cup sauerkraut
8   slices rye bread
½   cup butter, softened
4   slices corned beef
4   slices Swiss cheese
Russian Dressing (optional)

Rinse the sauerkraut under warm running water to remove the excess salt and drain on paper towels.

Spread the bread with butter, and on 4 slices layer the following: 1 slice of corned beef, ¼ cup sauerkraut, 1 slice of Swiss cheese. Spread on a spoonful or two of Russian dressing, if desired. Top with the remaining bread. Spread the outside of the sandwich with butter and cook in a skillet over moderate heat until golden on both sides.

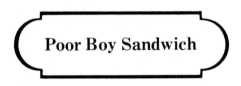

Poor Boy Sandwich

(4 servings)

1   long loaf Italian bread
Butter or Mayonnaise
¼   cup olive oil mixed with oregano and basil to taste
4   slices ham or prosciutto
4   slices mortadella or salami
4   slices provolone or Swiss cheese
1   large tomato, sliced thin
Lettuce

Cut the loaf of bread in half lengthwise and spread the bottom half with butter or mayonnaise. Drizzle the olive oil over the top half.

Arrange the ham slices as a first layer on the bottom half of the bread. Add a layer of mortadella, a layer of cheese, and a layer of tomato and lettuce. Cover with the top half of the bread and cut the loaf into fourths.

Jacques Pépin's Herbed Tomato Sandwich

(4 servings)

1   loaf French bread, about 10 inches long, sliced lengthwise
1   clove garlic, split
1½ tablespoons olive oil
3   tomatoes, sliced
1   tablespoon finely chopped fresh basil
1   small red onion, very thinly sliced
Salt and freshly ground black pepper

Rub the inside of both halves of the bread with the split clove of the garlic, so that the garlic flavors the bread lightly, and drizzle on 1 tablespoon of the olive oil. Arrange the tomato slices down the length of half the loaf and sprinkle generously with fresh basil. Arrange the onion slices over the tomatoes. Season with salt and pepper. Drizzle a little more olive oil over all to moisten. Carefully close the sandwich by pressing the two halves of the loaf together. Wrap the sandwich tightly in foil or plastic wrap, and leave for 30 minutes, to combine and "ripen" the flavors. Slice into fourths.

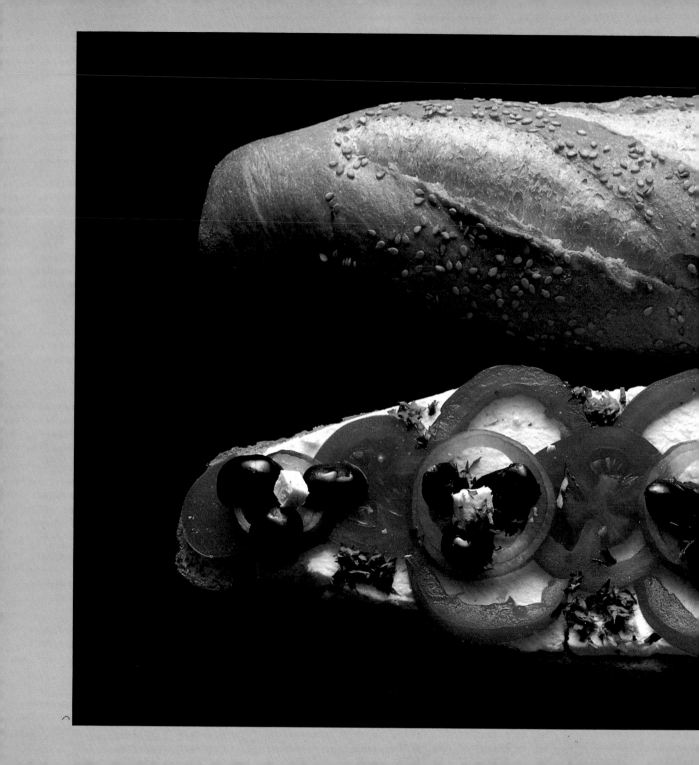

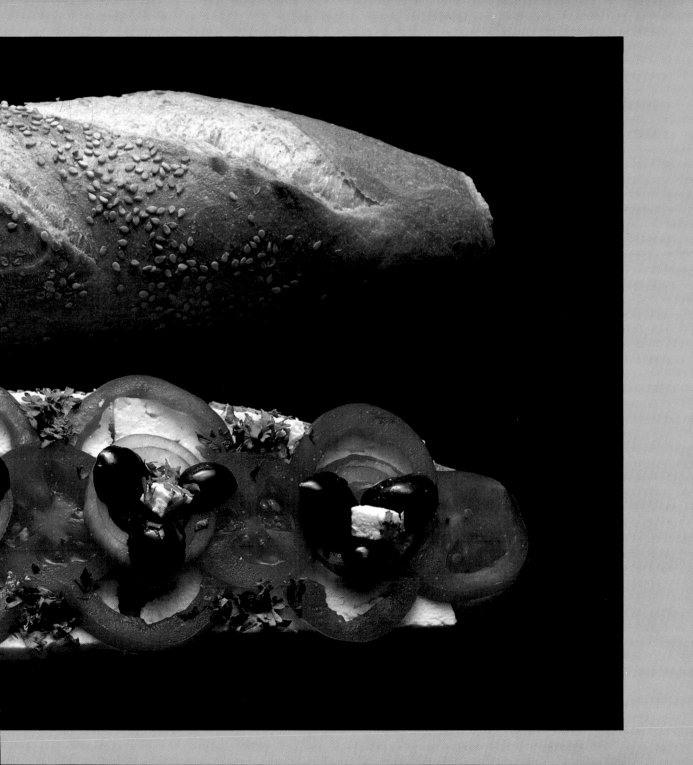

Michael Batterberry's Greek Salad Hero

(4 servings)

1 loaf Italian or French bread, about 8-12 inches long, sliced lengthwise
3 tablespoons olive oil
½ pound feta cheese, drained if waterpacked, and sliced ¼ inch thick
3-4 tomatoes, thinly sliced
1 small red onion, sliced and separated into rings
⅓ cup oil-cured black olives (Greek, if possible), cut in half, with pits removed
4 sprigs parsley, finely chopped
Salt and freshly ground black pepper

Brush the bottom half of the loaf with olive oil and arrange slices of feta cheese down the length. Top the feta with slices of tomato, rings of onion, and olives. Garnish with chopped parsley, add salt and pepper, and close the sandwich. Slice into fourths.

Ham & Crab Rolls

(4 sandwiches)

½ pound crab meat
½ cup Mayonnaise
½ cup diced celery
½ tablespoon chopped parsley
1 tablespoon fresh lemon juice
Tabasco sauce
Worcestershire sauce
Salt and freshly ground black pepper
4 French or other crusty-type rolls, split; or 1 long loaf French or Italian bread, split lengthwise and cut into fourths
¼ cup butter, melted
4 slices Danish ham

Preheat the oven to 350°

Mix the crab with the mayonnaise, celery, parsley, and lemon juice. Add Tabasco, Worcestershire sauce, salt, and black pepper to taste. Blend well.

Brush both halves of each roll with the melted butter and place them, open, in the oven. Toast lightly, remove from oven, and top each with a slice of ham spread lengthwise across the opened-up rolls. Spoon crab filling onto the ham on the bottom half of the roll and fold the other half of the ham and the roll to top.

(Preceding pages) **Greek salad hero**

Fried Oyster Hero with Hot Sauce

(4 servings)

24 oysters, shucked
Cayenne
Freshly ground black pepper
2 eggs
½ cup milk
1½ cups fresh bread crumbs, finely ground, and seasoned with salt and pepper
1 long loaf French or Italian bread
¼ cup butter, melted
1 cup vegetable oil
Hot sauce (optional, *see* recipe below)

Preheat the oven to 350°.

Pat the oysters dry with paper towels and sprinkle lightly with cayenne and black pepper. Beat the eggs with the milk and spread the bread crumbs on a large plate or piece of waxed paper. Dip the oysters 1, at a time, in the beaten eggs, then in the bread crumbs. Set aside.

Split the bread lengthwise. Pull out a strip of soft bread 2″ wide and 1″ deep down the length of the bottom half of the loaf. Brush both halves of the loaf with melted butter and lightly brown in the oven.

Meanwhile, heat the vegetable oil in a 10″ skillet. When the oil is hot, sauté the oysters quickly, 6 or so at a time. Remove from the skillet with a slotted spoon and transfer to paper towels to drain.

To assemble the oyster hero, spread hot sauce on both halves of the bread, arrange the oysters down the hollowed-out strip, and top with lettuce. Close the loaf and cut into fourths.

Hot Sauce:
¼ cup chili sauce
¼ cup ketchup
1½ tablespoons horseradish
2 teaspoons lemon juice
¼ teaspoon Worcestershire sauce
Tabasco sauce to taste
Freshly ground black pepper

Whisk all together in a small bowl, or shake together in a jar.

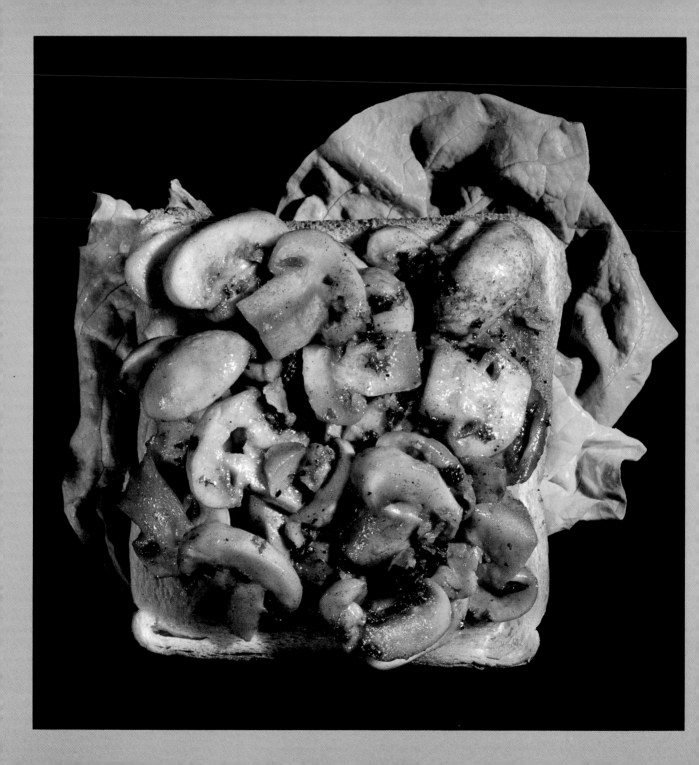

Knife & Fork
Sandwiches

Preparing one of these entrées might seem like going to a lot of trouble for just a sandwich—but these are not just sandwiches. They are meals. Some are elegant, some hearty, some absolutely melt-in-your-mouth delicious. These are sandwiches of ballottine of sole and salmon, sandwiches of ratatouille and of steak tartare, Italian fried cheese, and French-toasted cream cheese sandwiches. A few of the recipes are complicated; several require a good deal of preparation. But when the results are in, they are well worth the effort.

Advance organization helps: read the recipe carefully, see what ingredients are needed, and only leave for the last minute (the day you plan to serve) the buying of ingredients that are best when very fresh, such as chicken livers, mushrooms, ground meat, or seafood.

Prepare what you can ahead of time. You'll be able to cook and serve in a much more relaxed frame of mind—even to sit down and enjoy the meal with your guests—if the final steps are few in number and relatively easy. To take Chicken Livers & Mushroom Sandwiches as an example, you can complete in advance all the steps right up to cooking the livers themselves. Then you need only sauté the livers (a quick process) and return the other ingredients to the pan to warm them before serving. Make the toast while the sauce is thickening in the pan. The Ballottine of Sole and Salmon is made the day before you plan to serve it. And Hollandaise for Eggs Benedict can be made ahead and warmed at the last moment. There is one sandwich, however, that should only be prepared immediately before serving: Tartare Toasts. You can do any slicing, chopping, or measuring of the other ingredients beforehand, but the meat should not be handled until just before you're ready to eat it. At that point, mix the meat with the seasonings, spread it on the toast, add the egg yolks, place on plates, and bring to the table. Steak tartare's main ingredient is raw beef, and its subtle and delicate flavor will be best when the meat is very fresh.

Mushroom sauté on toast

Ratatouille Sandwiches

(4 sandwiches)

- ½ cup all-purpose flour
- 1 medium eggplant, peeled and cut into cubes
- ¼ cup olive oil
- 1 medium onion, chopped
- ½ clove garlic, crushed
- ½ teaspoon sweet basil
- ½ teaspoon oregano
- 1 teaspoon salt
- Freshly ground black pepper
- 1½ cups canned Italian plum tomatoes
- 2 tablespoons chopped parsley
- Capers
- 4 English muffins, split
- 8 slices Muenster cheese
- Freshly grated Parmesan cheese

Preheat the broiler.

Lightly flour the eggplant cubes. Heat the olive oil along with the onion, garlic, basil, oregano, salt, and pepper in a skillet over moderate heat. Add the floured cubes of eggplant, cover, and cook for 20 minutes, or until the eggplant is tender. Stir frequently. Add the tomatoes and cook uncovered 10 minutes more, stirring frequently. Add parsley and capers.

Butter the English muffins and toast under the broiler. Then cover each with a slice of Muenster and run under the broiler again, until the cheese melts. Heap on the ratatouille. The ratatouille may also be served at room temperature on black bread. Sprinkle with freshly grated Parmesan cheese.

Mushroom Sauté on Toast

(4 open-face sandwiches)

- 4 tablespoons Garlic Butter or 4 tablespoons butter and ½ clove garlic, crushed
- ½ pound medium size mushrooms, thinly sliced
- 4 slices white bread, toasted
- Finely chopped parsley

Melt the garlic butter or the butter and garlic in a skillet over moderately high heat. When the butter has finished foaming, add the mushrooms. Toss them until they are coated with the butter and sauté to a golden brown.

Serve at once on toasted bread slices, spooning the remaining juices over each sandwich. Garnish with a sprinkling of parsley.

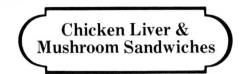

Chicken Liver & Mushroom Sandwiches

(2 open-face sandwiches)

- 1 pound chicken livers
- 2 tablespoons all-purpose flour
- 4 tablespoons butter
- ½ pound mushrooms, sliced
- 2 small onions, chopped
- ½ cup dry red wine
- 6 tablespoons chicken broth
- Salt and freshly ground black pepper
- 4 slices white bread
- 1 tablespoon finely chopped parsley

Cut each chicken liver into 4 pieces, removing any membrane or discolored spots. Dry the pieces with paper towels and roll them in the flour, shaking off all excess flour.

Melt 2 tablespoons of butter in a large skillet over medium heat. Add the mushrooms and sauté until wilted; remove from the pan and set aside. Melt the rest of the butter in the skillet, then add the onions, and cook until translucent. Add the chicken livers, turning them in the butter until they are well coated. Then sauté, stirring frequently, just until the livers are cooked through—when there is no trace of pink inside.

Return the mushrooms to the pan, add the red wine and the chicken broth, and stir until the sauce is smooth and slightly thickened. Season with salt and pepper to taste.

Toast the bread slices and spoon the chick-

en liver and mushroom mixture over them. Sprinkle with parsley.

Frosted Sandwich Cake

(12 servings)

- 1 loaf white bread, unsliced
- Mayonnaise
- Egg Salad
- 2-3 ripe tomatoes, sliced and seeded
- Shrimp and Artichoke Salad
- 1 bunch watercress
- Cream cheese, very softened

Trim the crusts from the bread and slice the loaf horizontally into 5 layers. Spread the bottom layer with egg salad, cover with the second layer of bread, and spread the bread with mayonnaise. Arrange tomato slices over the mayonnaise. Cover the tomatoes with the next layer of bread and spread the bread with Shrimp and artichoke salad. Cover the shrimp salad with the fourth layer of bread, and spread the bread with mayonnaise. Wash the watercress, pat it dry and remove the stems. Arrange watercress leaves over the mayonnaise and top with the last layer of bread. Frost the entire loaf with cream cheese and refrigerate, covered, until the cream cheese is firm. Slice the loaf vertically to serve it.

Kibbe Sandwiches

(4 open-face sandwiches)

½ cup bulghur wheat
¾ cup water
1 pound lean lamb (from the leg), ground once
½ clove garlic, crushed
12 fresh mint leaves, finely chopped
¼ teaspoon dried oregano
1 teaspoon finely chopped red onion
Salt and crushed black pepper to taste
4 slices dark pumpernickel bread, or 4 pitas

Cook the bulghur by bringing it to a boil in the water, then allowing it to sit, covered, for about 20 minutes, or until the water has been absorbed.

Place the meat in a large bowl and, using a fork, lightly mix in the garlic, mint, oregano, red onion, salt, and pepper. Then add the bulghur. The mixture should be a coarse one. Taste and adjust seasonings, if necessary.

Serve at room temperature on pumpernickel bread or in pita rounds.

Tartare Toasts

(2 open-face sandwiches)

12 ounces best quality lean round steak or sirloin steak, ground twice (the encasing fat should be cut off before the meat is ground)
1 tablespoon capers
3 tablespoons thinly sliced scallions, or finely chopped onion
1 tablespoon finely chopped parsley parsley
1 tablespoon Worcestershire sauce
2 teaspoons prepared mustard
4 anchovy fillets, chopped
Salt and freshly ground black pepper
2 slices rye bread, toasted
Butter
2 egg yolks

Place the meat in a large bowl and, using a fork, lightly mix in the capers, scallions, parsley, Worcestershire sauce, mustard, and anchovies. Add salt and pepper to taste. Shape the mixture into two thick patties and place each on a slice of buttered rye toast. Make a small well in each patty and drop in the egg yolk. Serve at once.

Veal Sandwiches Marengo

(4 open-face sandwiches)

- 2 tablespoons butter
- 1 tablespoon oil
- ¼ pound mushrooms, sliced
- 2 tablespoons white wine
- 2 tablespoons orange juice
- 4 slices white bread
- Orange Butter
- 3 tablespoons butter
- 2 tablespoons oil
- 8 thin veal scallops
- Flour
- Salt and freshly ground black pepper
- ⅓ cup black olives, cut in half, with pits removed
- 2 tablespoons chopped parsley

Melt the 2 tablespoons of butter and the tablespoon of oil in a skillet over high heat and sauté the mushroom slices until lightly browned. Add the white wine and let it bubble for a minute or so, then add the orange juice, stirring constantly until the liquid becomes slightly syrupy. Remove the pan from the heat.

Toast the bread and spread each slice with orange butter.

In a separate skillet melt butter and oil over high heat. Flour the veal scallops and season them with salt and pepper. When the butter in the skillet has stopped foaming, put as many scallops into the pan as will easily fit. Brown the scallops quickly on both sides and, as they are done, place each on a piece of buttered toast.

Return the skillet with the mushrooms in it to moderately high heat and stir briskly until sizzling. Spoon the mushroom slices over the top of the veal scallops. Garnish with black olives and a sprinkling of chopped parsley.

Mandarin Steak Sandwiches

(4 sandwiches)

- 1 pound London broil
- ½ cup soy sauce
- ½ cup water
- Sugar
- ⅓ cup dry red wine, *or* Scotch
- 8 slices sesame seed bread
- Butter
- Chopped parsley
- Prepared mustard (optional)

Place the London broil in a shallow pan.

In a small bowl, mix the soy sauce with the water and add sugar until the mixture tastes sweet. Stir in the wine or Scotch and pour over the meat. Marinate for at least 3 hours.

Preheat the broiler.

Broil the meat to the desired doneness, then slice it very thin. Toast the bread, butter it, and arrange the meat over 4 slices of bread. Sprinkle with chopped parsley, dab on a bit of mustard, if desired, and top with the remaining bread.

Cold Chicken Sandwiches Warmed with Gingery Sauce

(2 open-face sandwiches)

1 chicken breast, skinned, boned, and split
Salt and white pepper
3 tablespoons butter
2 slices white bread
2 lettuce leaves

Ginger Sauce:
4 tablespoons soy sauce
2 tablespoons honey
1 clove garlic, crushed
½ teaspoon salt
3 tablespoons peanut oil
2 scallions, chopped fine
5 thin slices fresh gingerroot, finely chopped
½ teaspoon crushed red pepper

Preheat the oven to 400°.

Sprinkle the halves of the chicken breast with salt and pepper. Melt 2 tablespoons of butter in a casserole (one that has a lid) over moderately high heat. When the butter is foaming, add the chicken breasts, roll them in the butter to coat all over, then remove the casserole from the heat. Spread 1 tablespoon of butter on a sheet of waxed paper and place it buttered side down on the chicken. Cover the casserole and put it in the oven for about 5 minutes. When the chicken feels firm to the touch, it is done. Allow the chicken to cool completely, then slice it horizontally.

Combine the soy sauce, honey, garlic, and salt in a small bowl and let the mixture stand for 5 minutes. In a small saucepan over low heat, warm the oil, scallions, gingerroot, and red pepper for 3 minutes. Pour the contents of the saucepan into the mixture in the bowl and blend well.

Toast the bread, place a leaf of lettuce on each slice, and arrange slices of cold chicken on top. Spoon the warmed sauce over all.

Mozzarella in Carrozza

(4 sandwiches)

8 slices white bread
8 thin slices mozzarella
4 eggs
3 tablespoons milk
Salt and freshly ground black pepper
Fine dry bread crumbs
Oil for frying

Anchovy Sauce (optional):
¼ cup butter or margarine
1 tablespoon chopped anchovies
2 teaspoons finely chopped parsley
1 teaspoon capers, chopped
1 teaspoon fresh lemon juice

If serving the anchovy sauce with these sandwiches, prepare it first: Melt the butter or margarine over low heat in a small saucepan and stir in the anchovies, parsley, capers, and lemon juice. Keep the sauce warm until the sandwiches are ready to serve.

Using a 3″ cookie or pastry cutter, cut the bread, 2 slices at a time, into 3″ circles.

Make sandwiches of the bread and cheese, centering 2 slices of mozzarella between 2 bread rounds. The slices of cheese should be slightly smaller than the circles of bread.

Beat together the eggs, milk, salt and pepper. Spread bread crumbs on a large plate or sheet of waxed paper. Dip each sandwich in the egg mixture and then roll the edges, wheel-like, in the bread crumbs. This is to seal in the cheese.

Fry the sandwiches in a large, oiled skillet until brown on both sides. Drain on paper towels and serve while still hot, spooning anchovy sauce on top, if desired.

Croque-monsieur

(4 sandwiches)

8 tablespoons butter
½ pound mushrooms, sliced
8 slices bacon
4 slices Swiss cheese
8 slices white bread
4 eggs
3 tablespoons milk
Salt and freshly ground black pepper

Melt 2 tablespoons of butter in a large skillet over moderately high heat and sauté the sliced mushrooms until they are soft. In another skillet fry the bacon and drain on paper towels.

Place single slices of cheese on 4 slices of bread. Add a layer of sautéed mushrooms and crumble bacon on top. Cover with a second slice of bread, pressing the edges together to seal slightly.

Beat together the eggs, milk, salt, and pepper and dip each sandwich into the mixture. Melt the remaining butter in a large skillet over moderately high heat and when the butter is foaming add the sandwiches. Sauté until brown on both sides.

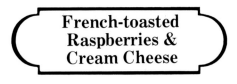

French-toasted Raspberries & Cream Cheese

(2 sandwiches)

4 slices white bread
1 3-ounce package cream cheese, softened
Raspberry preserves or jam
4 eggs
3 tablespoons milk
4 tablespoons butter

Spread 2 slices of bread with a thick layer of cream cheese, cover with a layer of preserves, and top with the remaining 2 slices of bread. Press the edges together.

Beat the eggs with the milk and dip each sandwich into the mixture. Melt the butter in a large skillet over moderately high heat and when the butter is foaming add the sandwiches. Sauté until brown on both sides.

Eggs Florentine

(4 servings)

1 10-ounce package frozen chopped spinach
2 tablespoons butter
Nutmeg
2 tablespoons cream
Salt and freshly ground black pepper
4 eggs
4 slices white bread, or 2 English muffins, split
Paprika

Cook the spinach according to package directions until tender but still green. Then put it in a fine strainer and push out all the water. Melt the butter in a saucepan and add a pinch of nutmeg and the spinach. Using a wooden spoon, stir the mixture over medium heat, gradually adding the cream. Stir constantly until the mixture begins to boil, then reduce heat to low. Let simmer for 1 minute, then add salt and pepper to taste.

To serve, poach the eggs and toast the bread. Spoon a liberal amount of spinach on each slice of toast and top with a poached egg. Garnish with paprika.

WITH BACON: Before adding the poached egg, sprinkle the spinach with crumbled bacon.

Eggs Benedict

(2 servings)

Hollandaise Sauce:
  4 egg yolks
  1 tablespoon fresh lemon juice
  ¼ teaspoon salt
  Cayenne
  ½ cup butter, softened
  ¼ cup boiling water

  4 slices Canadian bacon
  1 tablespoon butter
  2 English muffins, split
  2 tablespoons butter
  4 eggs
  Salt
  1 teaspoon vinegar
  Paprika

Preheat the broiler.

Make the hollandaise sauce first: Put the egg yolks, lemon juice, salt, and a dash of cayenne pepper in the container of a blender or food processor. Blend until smooth. Add the softened butter and boiling water and blend until homogenized (the secret of this sauce is having all the ingredients well blended before it is cooked).

With a spatula, transfer the liquid sauce to the top of a small double boiler. There should be a small amount of boiling water in the bottom of the double boiler, but it must not touch the upper pot.

Cook the sauce over medium heat, stirring constantly with the spatula and scraping the bottom and the sides until the sauce thickens to the desired consistency. If the sauce begins to thicken too quickly, remove the top of the double boiler and keep stirring off the heat. Place over warm water until ready to use.

Sauté the Canadian bacon in 1 tablespoon butter until lightly browned on both sides.

Toast the English muffins under the broiler. Remove from the oven, turn off the heat, and place 4 plates in the oven to warm. Butter the muffins and cover each half with a slice of Canadian bacon.

Poach the eggs in salted water to which the vinegar has been added (the vinegar helps to coagulate the egg white). When the eggs are cooked to the desired point, remove them with a slotted spoon, pausing a moment over paper towels to let the excess water drain. Slide the poached eggs on top of the Canadian bacon, place each muffin on a heated plate, and spoon on the hollandaise. Sprinkle with paprika and serve.

Smoked Salmon & Egg Sandwiches

(4 sandwiches)

- 8 eggs
- 4 tablespoons water
- ¼ pound smoked salmon, chopped
- 1 tablespoon minced parsley

Freshly ground black pepper

Butter

- 4 slices pumpernickel

Butter

Chopped fresh chives

Beat the eggs with the water and add the salmon, parsley, and pepper. Melt the butter in a large skillet over low heat; when it begins to foam, add the egg mixture. Stir with a wooden spoon, scraping the bottom and sides of the skillet until the eggs are thick and creamy. Remove from heat before the eggs are done—they will continue cooking in the pan. Toast the bread, spread with butter, and spoon the eggs on top. Garnish with a sprinkling of chopped chives.

Sardines Diable

(4 servings)

- 1 tablespoon Dijon mustard
- 4 tablespoons ketchup
- 1 tablespoon capers, chopped
- 1 tablespoon chopped parsley
- 1 tablespoon fresh lemon juice
- 3 ¾-ounce cans sardines, packed in olive oil
- 1½ tablespoons butter

Salt and freshly ground black pepper

- ½ teaspoon dried thyme
- 8 slices white bread

Finely chopped parsley

In a small bowl mix together the mustard, ketchup, capers, parsley, and lemon juice. Set aside. Place the sardines in a strainer, rinse off all the oil under gently running hot water, and drain on paper towels.

Melt the butter in a skillet over moderately high heat and add the drained sardines, carefully turning them in the butter until heated through. Sprinkle on salt, pepper, and thyme. Pour in the mustard/ketchup mixture and stir until heated. Toast the bread and place 1 slice on each of 4 plates. Cut the remaining slices diagonally into fourths and arrange 4 toast points around the slice of toast on each plate. Serve the sardine mixture over the toast and garnish with chopped parsley.

André Soltner's Seafood Ballottine Sandwiches

(8-10 open-face sandwiches)

To assemble:
- 2 tablespoons watercress leaves,
- ½ tablespoon finely chopped parsley
- 8-10 slices white bread, with crusts removed
- 5 tablespoons mayonnaise, preferably homemade
- Cherry tomatoes, quartered, with seeds removed
- Olives, cut into slivers (optional)

Prepare the *ballottine* at least one day in advance. (A *ballottine* is a type of galantine, in this case made of fish, that is stuffed and rolled.)

Blanch the watercress leaves in boiling water for 2 minutes. Drain, refresh under cold water, and purée by passing through a fine sieve. Add the purée and the parsley to the mayonnaise and blend well.

Cut the bread into rounds. Mask each piece of bread with a smooth layer of the green mayonnaise. Slice the *ballottine* and center a slice on each piece of bread. Garnish with cherry tomatoes and slivers of olive.

Ballottine of Sole & Salmon

(*Ballottine* for 8-10 sandwiches)

Mousseline:
- 1 pound fillets of sole
- 3 eggs
- 1½ cups heavy cream
- 1 teaspoon salt
- White pepper

- 2 pounds fillets of sole
  Salt
- ½ pound fresh salmon, cut into finger-sized strips
- 2 quarts fish stock

Prepare the mousseline, first making sure all the ingredients are very cold: Grind the pound of sole in a blender in batches until it is a very fine purée. Add the eggs, cream, salt, and pepper to taste.

Wet and squeeze out a kitchen towel and lay it flat on a table. Place a piece of waxed paper over it and cut it so it is the same size as the towel. Carefully place the 2 pounds of whole fillets of sole on the paper, laying them flat. Season with salt.

Spread the mousseline over the fillets. Place the salmon fingers in the middle of each fillet.

Carefully roll the fillets with mousseline and salmon into a cylinder shape, pushing the fish away from the waxed paper as you go.

(Preceding pages) Seafood ballottine sandwich, avocado-shrimp sandwich

The cylinder should emerge compact. Remove the waxed paper, center the *ballottine* on the towel or cheesecloth, and tie securely at each end and in the center.

Place the *ballottine* in a pot, cover with fish stock, and simmer slowly for 30 minutes. Cool overnight in the stock.

Michael Batterberry's Avocado-Shrimp Sandwiches

(6 open-face sandwiches)

Guacamole:
- 1 medium avocado
- 1 teaspoon fresh lime juice or lemon juice
- 1 tablespoon finely chopped fresh coriander
- ½ small chili pepper, seeded and chopped fine

- 1 pound shrimp, shelled and deveined, with tails removed
- ¾ cup olive oil
- 6 tablespoons fresh lime juice
- Salt and freshly ground black pepper
- 1 avocado
- 6 slices white bread, toasted, with crusts removed
- Fresh coriander
- 1 lemon, sliced thin and quartered (optional)

Prepare the guacamole: Split the avocado, remove the seed, and spoon out the flesh and mash coarsely with lime or lemon juice. Blend in the coriander and chili pepper. Refrigerate until ready to use.

Plunge the shrimp into 2 quarts of boiling water and cook just until pink. Drain immediately and refresh under cold water to stop further cooking.

In a large glass or enamel bowl, mix the oil with the lime juice and toss the shrimp in the mixture. Season with salt and pepper and let marinate for 1 hour or more. Drain when ready to use.

Peel the avocado and slice it thin. Sprinkle all exposed surfaces with lemon juice to prevent darkening.

To assemble the sandwiches, spread each slice of toast with an even layer of guacamole and arrange alternating rows of shrimp and sliced avocado. Garnish, if you wish, with coriander and quarters of lemon slices.

Backyard Buffets

Although the pita sandwiches on the following pages are portable, most of this elegant outdoor fare would not travel well. Open-face sandwiches are just not packable. Neither are tacos. But what if they only had to travel out to your own backyard? This chapter offers a sampler of splendid sandwiches for a backyard buffet.

At first blush tacos may not seem like food for buffet or backyard either, but really they lend themselves very well to a festive set-up. Lay a table with all the ingredients and let the guests assemble their own. Put warm tortillas in a pretty basket lined with a print cloth or napkin. Keep the meat fillings hot in separate chafing dishes or fondue pots. Set out bowls of shredded lettuce, chopped onion, sour cream, and grated cheeses; and plates of sliced tomatoes and avocados (sprinkle with lemon juice to prevent darkening). And pitchers of taco or chili sauce and salsa fria. The same kind of assembly-line set-up works for the pita sandwiches, too.

And imagine how spectacular a table would look spread with a magnificent arrangement of perfectly-prepared open-face sandwiches. Accompany them with an assortment of pickles and relishes and a big bowl of homemade coleslaw (see page 210).

Many of the sandwiches included here are highly spiced. A hearty iced tea would go well with any of them—and very cold beer is a wonderful partner for the smørrebrøds and the tacos, especially.

Round out your backyard buffet with a spectacular cake for a special occasion, with baskets of fresh summer fruits, or with a compote of melon balls (perhaps mixed with blueberries) or cut fresh grapes, pitted cherries, and slices of fresh peach.

Rolled ham sandwich, artichoke sandwich

Richard Sax's Rolled Ham Sandwiches

(4 open-face sandwiches)

Egg filling:
- 4 hard-boiled eggs, chopped
- ¼ cup Mayonnaise
- ½ teaspoon Dijon mustard
- ¼ cup mango (or other) chutney

- 2 hard-boiled eggs, chopped
- 1 tablespoon finely chopped parsley
- 4 thin slices whole wheat bread, with crusts removed
- 2-3 teaspoons Dijon mustard
- 4 thin slices Jarlsberg cheese or any good Swiss-type cheese
- 8 thin slices Smithfield ham or Westphalian ham, *or* prosciutto

Prepare the egg filling: Place the eggs, mayonnaise, mustard, and chutney in a bowl and blend well.

Spread the bread with a thin layer of mustard and cut the slices of cheese and ham to fit the bread. Lay a slice of cheese on each piece of bread.

For each sandwich, take 2 slices of ham and lay them flat. At one end of each slice, place a small scoop of the egg filling. Carefully roll up each slice to enclose the filling. Smooth the ends and lay the two stuffed ham rolls, seam side down, on top of the cheese at either side of the sandwich.

Sprinkle a mixture of hard-boiled egg and chopped parsley down the center of the sandwich, between the 2 stuffed ham rolls. Decorate with ribbons of cheese.

Richard Sax's Ham & Cheese Sandwiches

(4 open-face sandwiches)

- 4 thin slices whole wheat bread, with crusts removed
- 4 teaspoons unsalted butter
- 4 teaspoons Dijon mustard
- ½ cup mango chutney
- 4 slices Smithfield ham or Westphalian ham, *or* prosciutto
- 4 slices Jarlsberg cheese or any good Swiss-type cheese

Parsley sprigs

Spread the bread with a thin layer of butter and then mustard. Spread on a layer of chutney, arranging any large pieces of mango as smoothly as possible. For each sandwich, trim a slice of ham and a slice of cheese to fit the bread. Lay the cheese on top of the chutney layer. Roll up the ham slice loosely and center it on top of the cheese. Garnish with sprigs of fresh parsley.

Michael Batterberry's Artichoke Sandwiches

(2 open-face sandwiches)

2 teaspoons mayonnaise, preferably homemade
½-1 teaspoon Dijon mustard
2 thin slices whole wheat or white bread, with crusts removed
1 6-ounce jar oil-packed artichoke hearts, sliced
1 tomato, peeled, seeded, and cut into slivers
2 hard-boiled eggs, coarsely chopped
2 teaspoons capers, drained
1 teaspoon finely chopped parsley

Combine the mayonnaise and mustard to taste and spread thinly on the bread. Lay the artichoke slices in a strip diagonally across the bread. Add strips of tomato next to the artichoke hearts. Add the chopped egg on either side of the tomato. Garnish with capers and parsley.

Felafel

(4 servings)

2 cups cooked chick-peas
1 cup bread crumbs
¼ cup sesame paste (tahini)
¼ cup soy sauce (tamari)
3 tablespoons finely chopped parsley
½ teaspoon ground cumin
½ teaspoon ground coriander
2 cloves garlic, crushed
4 tablespoons oil
4 pitas
Tahini dressing (*see* recipe below)

Purée the chick-peas in a food processor, blender, or food mill. Combine the purée with the other ingredients and chill for 1 hour before shaping into 4 patties.

Heat the oil in a skillet and fry the felafel over moderately high heat until browned on both sides. Drain on paper towels.

Serve in pita bread and top with tahini dressing.

Tahini Dressing:
¼ cup water
½ cup oil
¼ cup sesame paste (tahini)
¼ cup fresh lemon juice
2 tablespoons soy sauce (tamari)
1 clove garlic, minced

Whisk all together in a small bowl.

Maurice Moore-Betty's Curried Fish Pitas

(6 servings)

Curried Fish Stuffing:

10-12	ounces white or smoked fish fillets
1	cup milk
3	cups cooked rice, hot
4	tablespoons unsweetened butter
4	hard-boiled eggs, chopped
½	cup toasted pignola nuts
¾	teaspoon curry powder
2	tablespoons all-purpose flour
	Salt and pepper

6 pitas

Put fish in small saucepan, cover with milk, and bring to a boil. Reduce heat to low and cover. Simmer until fish flakes easily. Remove fish and break it into large chunks. Reserve the milk.

In a large bowl mix fish with rice. Stir in chopped eggs, pignola nuts, and 2 tablespoons of butter. Set aside.

Melt remaining 2 tablespoons of butter in a saucepan over low heat. Stir in curry powder and cook a minute or two to remove any acrid taste. Stir in flour and cook gently for 2 to 3 minutes without coloring. Stir in reserved milk and simmer 2 to 3 minutes more. Stir sauce into fish mixture. Spoon into pitas.

Maurice Moore-Betty's Hot Vegetable Pitas

(4 servings)

1	large garlic clove
1	teaspoon salt
⅓	cup olive oil
2	large onions, thinly sliced
1	medium eggplant, scored and sliced crosswise into ½-inch strips
	Salt and freshly ground black pepper
1	teaspoon paprika
2	red or green bell peppers, thinly sliced
3-4	firm, ripe tomatoes, peeled, seeded, and thickly sliced
1	cup drained cooked chick-peas
½	cup finely chopped Italian (flat) parsley

Mash garlic to a paste with the salt. Heat 3 tablespoons of oil in a skillet and sauté the onions and garlic until golden. Sprinkle eggplant with salt and let drain for 30 minutes.

Preheat the oven to 350°. Spread onion mixture in a baking dish and add salt and pepper to taste and some paprika. Arrange in alternating layers the eggplant, pepper, and tomatoes, sprinkling salt, pepper, and paprika among them. Drizzle the remaining oil on top.

Bake 1½ hours, or until the vegetables are tender. Stir in the chick-peas and parsley and spoon into the pitas.

Stuffed pitas: curried fish, hot vegetable

Beef Tacos with Salsa Fria

(6 servings)

- 5 tablespoons vegetable oil
- 1 pound ground beef
- 6 tortillas
- 12 thin slices Cheddar cheese
- 2 medium Bermuda onions, finely chopped
- 2 tomatoes, sliced
- Shredded lettuce
- Mexican Salsa Fria or taco sauce
- Avocado slices (optional)
- Sour cream (optional)

Heat 1 tablespoon of oil in a skillet over moderately high heat. Add the ground beef, breaking up the meat with a fork. Stir until cooked, then remove from the heat.

In a separate skillet heat the remaining oil to sizzling and fry each tortilla quickly until limp. Cover half of each tortilla with 2 slices of cheese, folding the uncovered half over the top of the cheese. Fry on both sides until golden.

To serve, open the tortillas and stuff with cooked hamburger meat, chopped onion, shredded lettuce, and tomato slices. Pour on a little salsa fria or taco sauce and garnish with slices of avocado and spoonfuls of sour cream.

Sausage-stuffed Tacos

(4 servings)

- 4 tablespoons vegetable oil
- ½ pound smoked, spiced pork sausage, skinned and chopped
- 2 tablespoons Mexican Salsa Fria or chili sauce
- 2 tablespoons freshly grated Parmesan cheese
- 4 tortillas
- 4 tablespoons finely chopped onion

Heat 1 tablespoon of oil in a skillet over moderately high heat. Add the chopped sausage and fry until lightly browned, about 5 minutes. Remove from the skillet with a slotted spoon and drain on paper towels. In a small bowl mix the cooked sausage meat with the salsa fria or chili sauce and the Parmesan cheese.

In a separate skillet heat the remaining 3 tablespoons of oil to sizzling. Drop in the tortillas, 1 at a time, and fry quickly until limp.

To serve, distribute the sausage mixture over the 4 tortillas, add a tablespoon of chopped onions to each, and then roll up the tortillas.

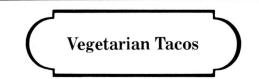

Vegetarian Tacos

(10-12 servings)

1	head lettuce, torn into bits
3	medium tomatoes, chopped
1	large white or red onion, thinly sliced
1	large zucchini, unpeeled and thinly sliced
6	radishes, red or white, thinly sliced
¼	head red cabbage, thinly sliced, then coarsely chopped (optional)
10-12	pitted green olives, drained and sliced (optional)
10-12	pitted black olives, drained and sliced (optional)
1	medium green or red bell pepper, finely chopped (optional)
10-15	mushrooms, sliced and sprinkled with lemon juice to retain whiteness (optional)
1	medium carrot, finely grated (optional)
10-12	tortillas
	Oil
½	pound Monterey Jack cheese, crumbled, or Cheddar cheese, crumbled, or mixture of the two (optional)

Grated Parmesan cheese (optional)
Green taco sauce, *or* favorite salad dressing

Prepare the vegetables, choosing the combination you wish to serve.

Pour oil to a depth of ¼ inch into a skillet large enough to accommodate a tortilla with room enough to turn it. Heat the oil to sizzling and lightly sauté each tortilla on both sides until it begins to brown, but remove from the oil while it is still limp enough to fold. Fold over slightly before draining so that the tortilla does not stiffen flat. Keep warm until all are prepared.

Stuff the slightly folded tacos with vegetables and fold over more firmly. Sprinkle with crumbled cheese and top with taco sauce or dressing.

Old Denmark's Smoked Salmon Smørrebrød

(2 open-face sandwiches)

- 2 thin slices square black bread, with crusts removed
- 1-2 teaspoons unsalted butter
- 4 thin slices smoked salmon
- 8 fresh asparagus, cooked just until tender and cooled to room temperature or canned asparagus
- 2 sprigs fresh dill
- 1 thin slice lemon, quartered

Spread the bread with a thin layer of butter. Place a slice of salmon at either side of the bread and lay 4 asparagus spears across the middle, between the slices of salmon. Trim the salmon to fit the bread. Decorate with a sprig of fresh dill and lemon quarters.

W. Peter Prestcott's Herring Sandwiches

(4 open-face sandwiches)

- 4 thin slices square black bread or pumpernickel, with crusts removed
- 2-3 teaspoons unsalted butter
- 4 marinated herring fillets
- 1 apple, cored and sliced crosswise into thin rounds
- 1 small red onion, thinly sliced
- ¼ cup sour cream
- 4 sprigs fresh dill

Spread the bread with a thin layer of butter. Arrange the herring fillets to cover the bread, cutting to fit. Place 2 slices of apple over the herring so that they fit neatly. Separate the onion slices into rings and arrange attractively across the apples, overlapping slightly. Top each apple slice with a small dollop of sour cream and a sprig of fresh dill.

(Preceding pages) Open-face smørrebrød: smoked salmon and asparagus, herring with apple and onion, sardines with onion and dill

Miriam Ungerer's "Poker Face from a Lady"

(2 open-face sandwiches)

2   thin slices square rye bread, with crusts removed
1-2 teaspoons Mayonnaise
1   3¾-ounce can boneless, skinless sardines
1   red onion, 1½″ in diameter, thinly sliced
Freshly ground black pepper
1   thin slice lemon, quartered
2   sprigs fresh dill (optional)

Spread the bread with a thin layer of mayonnaise and lay the sardines evenly over the top. Separate the onion slices into rings and lay on top of the sardines, overlapping slightly. Season with freshly ground black pepper and garnish with lemon quarters, and dill.

Smørrebrød with Pork & Prunes

(2 open-face sandwiches)

2 thin slices square rye or pumpernickel bread, with crusts removed
1 tablespoon unsalted butter, softened
6 very thin slices cold roast pork
2 thin slices orange
4 prunes, pitted

Spread the bread with a thin layer of butter. Arrange 3 slices of pork, one overlapping the other, to cover the bread. Make twists of the orange slices and center 1 on each sandwich. Place 2 prunes on each sandwich, 1 on either side of the twist.

Index